CW01645127

Cotswold Wildlife Park & Gardens

A gift from the
Cotswold Wildlife Park
&
Gardens
2015

Managing Director

Animal Curator

Rhinos on the Lawn

Rhinos on the Lawn

and the people who made the Cotswold Wildlife Park

by Matthew Jones

Rhinos on the Lawn
and the people who made the Cotswold Wildlife Park

First published in 2012

ISBN 978-1-905315-50-5

Main cover photograph by Andrew Lawson
Line drawings by Joanna Heyworth

Printed and bound by CPI Group (UK) Ltd, Croydon, CR0 4YY

Edited and designed by
Prepare to Publish Ltd, Charlbury, Oxfordshire
www.preparetopublish.com

Published by
Cotswold Wildlife Park
Burford, Oxfordshire OX18 4JP

Contents

Foreword by David Cameron, Prime Minister and MP for Witney

1 Before the beginning BRADWELL GROVE 1
2 "A constant battle with the builders" 1969-70 9
3 "Call this a wildlife park?" 1970-74 23
4 "Promoting a kindred spirit" 1975-80 41
5 "Improving on what we have got" 1980-1989 55
6 Accidents and achievements 1990-1999 69
7 "Don't do what is new: do what is never old" 2000-10 83

8 "Without them this would never have been possible" THE LIVES OF THE KEEPERS 101
9 "Planning the next generation's gardens" GROUNDS, GARDENS AND GARDENERS 115
10 Vital cogs STAFF BEHIND THE SCENES 127
11 Work and play LIVING AT THE PARK 135
12 Family charm CHILDREN AT THE PARK 143
13 "Learn something about animals and birds" EDUCATION AT THE PARK 151
14 "The best wildlife park that no one has ever heard of" PUBLIC RELATIONS AND PROMOTION 163

Conclusion 171
Notes 174
Index of names 178

Foreword

When Samantha and I first moved to the Cotswolds all those years ago, one of our first family explorations was to the Cotswold Wildlife Park. It was a trip down memory lane as we had both been there as children and had very happy memories of all it had to offer.

Enchanted by that first return visit, we have been back many times since, with our children, with our friends, and with our friends' children. Like the many visitors of all ages since the Park opened in 1970, our visits have allowed us to lose a few hours in the all-embracing beauty of nature, from the magnificent trees and gardens, to the endless variety and antics of the animals. More importantly, we come away from each visit with a greater appreciation of the vital importance of nature in all its forms, and of our responsibility to respect it, to work with it not against it, and to conserve it for future generations. Also, it keeps getting better: the 'Madagascar' exhibition is superb and I will never forget a lemur bouncing on the children's pram.

Having the Park in my constituency means that I have also occasionally had official dealings with it: I was invited to open the Park's new train station in 2007, a rare event for an MP. Two years later, the Park wrote to me about the bureaucracy involved in importing two young female white rhinos: I must have helped somehow, because one of them on her eventual arrival at the Park was named Nancy, after my daughter.

This book gives a voice to the community of dedicated people who have worked at the Park and made it what it is today, a source of joy and wonder to over a third of a million visitors every year. It is also a richly deserved tribute to the vision and determination of the Park's founder John Heyworth who, with all his staff past and present, can take pride in this special place.

David Cameron, Prime Minister and MP for Witney
January 2012

Chapter 1

Before the beginning

Bradwell Grove

Before the jungle of the Tropical House, the open 'African Plains' and the Madagascan wilderness of the Cotswold Wildlife Park, there was just an English agricultural estate, nestled on the edge of Oxfordshire. Bradwell Grove, close to the tranquil town of Burford, was the centre of an ancient parish predating the Norman Conquest, which also encompassed the communities of Holwell, Filkins and Broadwell. Surrounded by beautiful countryside and working farmland, it was nevertheless indistinguishable from hundreds of other estates across the country, governed by centuries of rural tradition and strict social hierarchy. While the Manor House and the huge 600-year-old oak beside it provide impressive physical links to past centuries, the cries of exotic animals and the shouts of delighted children which now echo across the acres were inconceivable for previous generations.

The current Manor House was established as the focal point of the Park's landscape over 200 years ago. In 1804, William Hervey, the estate's owner, commissioned William Atkinson to design a large residence in the Gothic style favoured by the aspiring and fashionable gentry of the era. Reminiscent of Horace Walpole's Strawberry Hill architecture at Twickenham, the turrets, parapets and arching bays provided a symbol of status which Hervey could display to his friends and peers. It was built by Richard Pace of nearby Lechlade on the site of a 17th century Jacobean building which had been mostly destroyed by fire. Part of this, however, was incorporated into the new north wing which accommodated servants. Extensions and outbuildings were added throughout the 19th century but the backdrop now integral to the beauty of the Park essentially remained the same.[1] Hervey died childless in 1863, so his grand home did not pass to any heirs. The estate was subsequently purchased in 1871 by Samuel Fox, an industrious ironmaster from Sheffield who had made his fortune by adapting the principle of crinoline dress frames for the production of umbrellas. It then passed to his son, William Henry Fox.

The recollections of local villager Norman G James offer a valuable insight into the workings of the house and estate under the latter 'Squire Fox'. The owner was described as looking "very like King George V... with a beard, and sturdily built".[2] The indoor household was headed by a butler and housekeeper, who strictly oversaw the work of several footmen and maids. The space currently used as the main office accommodated the housekeeper, while the neighbouring finance office housed the butler's pantry, complete with a strongroom to protect the silver. The first aid room under the stairs of the north wing once served as a pantry while the downstairs female toilets had a more unusual purpose as a 'smokeroom'. The traditional country sports of hunting and shooting were keenly pursued by Fox, requiring a stud groom, four tack men and two coachmen to manage the stables and coaches. Ten gardeners, five woodsmen and five gamekeepers cared for the grounds. A firm hierarchy governed the estate and "all employees and children were expected to salute by touching their caps or curtseying when meeting the Squire".[3] Such symbols of respect were continued by the estate staff well into the 20th century, even after the Wildlife Park had been established. This led to a clear distinction between an older generation of estate employees, called by their last name only, and the animal keepers of a more modern era.

The estate first entered the family of the present owners following the death of Fox in 1920, whereupon it was purchased by Colonel Cecil Francis Heyworth-Savage. Moving from the Grange in Toddington, Gloucestershire, he fulfilled all the expectations and duties of an English gentleman. The Colonel served as High Sheriff of Oxfordshire in 1929 and enjoyed hunting, shooting and fishing.[4] Norman James paints a portrait of a close community at its idyllic peak in the first decades of the 20th century. A well-maintained cricket pitch, for example, was situated close to the Park's entrance drive on an area now the car park, west of the llama paddock. Estate employees would often play local teams, with "proficiency in cricket [a] good recommendation for a job on the estate". Heyworth-Savage also entertained members of London society at home. He hosted shooting parties or arranged cricket matches between members of the Heythrop Hunt and one of the Guards' Regimental teams, after which strawberry cream teas would be served on the lawn.[5] Even this isolated rural tranquillity, however, could not avoid disruption by the long, arduous contest of the Second World War. Bradwell Grove Hospital was built to the north-east of the main house, and was used for nursing injured soldiers; troops were stationed close to Burford; piles of ammunition lined the by-roads among the nearby villages; and estate land was expropriated for conversion into an airfield.

John Heyworth

Colonel and Mrs Heyworth-Savage's only son, Lt. Colonel Reginald Heyworth, was killed in 1941, while in command of the 1st Royal Dragoons in North Africa. Along with the widespread impact of six years of war, this sparked a train of financial pressures and social transformation which eventually culminated in the birth of Cotswold Wildlife Park. When the Colonel died in 1949, the estate passed to Mr John Heyworth, his grandson and founder of the Park. Born in the Manor House and deeply attached to the family home, the new owner was unfortunately confronted with staggering death duties. Immediate and radical action was required in order to pay. Susan Heyworth, his wife, recollects a heart-breaking three-day auction of the house's fine furniture, as antique dealers flocked to the house like "jackdaws" and organised bidding rings to secure the goods at ruthlessly reduced prices.[6]

The Heyworths were left with an emptied house, which was very expensive to maintain. They moved to a smaller property on the estate and Mr Heyworth was forced to find a new purpose for the Manor. After a short-lived, unsuccessful attempt to establish Bradwell Grove as a film set, the building was rented to Oxford Regional

Hospital Board for 20 years. It was used to house staff for Bradwell Grove Hospital, but the new occupants failed to treat their accommodation kindly. Some portraits still remaining on the walls, for example, were used as dartboards and general maintenance was not upheld. By the late 1960s, the proud Manor, which had supported generations of bustling households, had fallen into a state of near-irreversible disrepair.

Boom-time for zoos

Around the same time, Britain's gradual economic recovery from the war, and the relative rise in disposable wealth, created the conditions for a boom in recreation. Increasing numbers of people had a greater amount of leisure time, while cars gave families the ability to venture further afield. A proliferation of zoos and animal attractions was a direct consequence of economic and social improvement. A contemporary article in *New Scientist* charted the development, stating that there were 20 zoos and bird gardens in the British Isles in 1950, 31 by 1960 and 95 by the end of 1969.[7] Cotswold Wildlife Park added to these figures when it opened to the public on 27 March 1970. Of course, not all of these ventures were as successful or enduring, but the foundation of the Park was embedded in this surge of public demand and consequent opportunities in the leisure industry. While by no means original as a business venture, the Park quickly began to distinguish itself from more profit-focused contemporaries. The purpose of the *New Scientist* article was to profile Scotia Investments Limited, whose business interests included bingo halls, Dudley Zoo and the zoo chain Associated Pleasure Parks. By contrast, there were "small personally-run zoos, typified by the excellent little Cotswold Wildlife Park... as much a way of life as a source of profit".[8] Several of the animal collections which emerged at the same time as the Wildlife Park, such as Twycross Zoo, Longleat Safari Park and Marwell Zoo, have grown to become globally successful and well-respected. The differences in their origins and trajectories, however, help to highlight the special virtues which have underpinned the Cotswold Wildlife Park since its foundation.

The work of Molly Badham, the founder (with Nathalie Evans) of Twycross Zoo in Warwickshire, was an inspiration to John Heyworth, with both establishing their respective attractions partly from the simple pleasure they derived from animals. Badham's zoo collection, however, emerged more spontaneously from an initially private interest, beginning with the famous Brooke Bond Tea chimpanzees and expanding to include capybaras, kinkajous, Chinese water deer and flamingos at a small bungalow in the countryside.[9] Word of mouth gradually spread knowledge of the collection until many families would turn up unexpectedly at weekends seeking admission. The decision was eventually made to move to larger, more convenient and purpose-bought premises in Twycross in 1962, with 22 acres opening to the public the following year. In order to attract more visitors, it came to exhibit larger exotic animals, including elephants and giraffes, requiring little more than basic planning permission for buildings. Badham's experiences highlight both the growing trend in emerging attractions of this nature and the lack of official regulation governing them. Her passion for animals led her to become one of the leading figures in the Federation of Zoological Gardens in Britain and Ireland, which began to improve zoo standards. She later led official inspections of Cotswold Wildlife Park on numerous occasions and gave very complimentary reports.

Longleat Lion Park, opening at Easter 1966, was the next significant new animal attraction of the period, establishing the modern concept of the safari park at the Marquis of Bath's stately home in Wiltshire. The brainchild of Jimmy Chipperfield, the circus proprietor and entertainer, Longleat was a commercial idea so revolutionary that it escaped the regulations of any existing planning laws. In his autobiography, Chipperfield described how he planned to release captive lions from their cages into open enclosures in the English countryside, where visitors, attracted by the spectacle and thrill of danger, could drive among them.[10] When the idea first became public, it was denounced as dangerous and anti-social, with *The Times* calling for government intervention to prevent the scheme. The venture proved so popular, however, that the capital costs were returned within four months of opening and the Park quickly expanded with additional drive-through enclosures. Similar Chipperfield enterprises swiftly followed at Woburn Abbey, Bedfordshire, and Knowsley, near Liverpool. Interest abroad was also aroused, leading to the establishment of safari parks in Holland,

Canada, France, Spain and Germany. John Heyworth considered seeking collaboration with the Chipperfields to help his own venture but was advised against surrendering his independent control. Fortunately this ensured millions of future visitors could experience walking, rather than driving, around the beautiful grounds surrounding the Manor House.[11]

Finally, John Knowles' venture at Marwell, Hampshire, was privately funded in a similar vein to the Cotswold Wildlife Park. Knowles, however, aimed to establish a wildlife collection following a strong conservation ethos, with a particular emphasis on rare hoofed animals such as the scimitar-horned oryx.[12] In a decision Knowles described as "totally crazy", the Marwell estate was purchased in 1969, providing free-draining paddocks, gently undulating landscape and suitable transport links.[13]

The only disadvantage was the presence of Marwell Hall, deemed unnecessary by Knowles as much as John Heyworth considered the Bradwell Grove Manor necessary to preserve. An outline planning application in May 1970 attracted hostility from neighbouring communities, fearing disruption caused by visitors travelling to the zoo. The Marwell plan, however, was strongly supported by the county council, which foresaw the potential for relieving tourist pressure from the increasingly congested New Forest, and the zoo was finally opened in the spring of 1972. Knowles sought to draw upon the best elements of Whipsnade Park Zoo in Bedfordshire, and Catskill Game Farm in New York, by providing spacious enclosures suiting the animals' needs yet ensuring visibility for the public with an open and attractive layout.[14] As a result, strong similarities could be drawn with the principles of Cotswold Wildlife Park. Both also shared the particularly brave and unusual decision to confound public demand by eschewing elephants, expected at all major animal attractions. Rather than fund inadequate facilities for these highly intelligent and complicated animals, they have remained absent since the beginning.

It was within this context, therefore, that the rejuvenation of Bradwell Grove was sparked; an explosion of public interest fuelled by economic and social improvement, which prompted a gradual shift in attitudes towards animal exhibitions. The commercial success experienced by Longleat was required to maintain a dilapidated Manor

House with a vibrant history, yet all profits were to be reinvested into improving the grounds, animal exhibits and enclosures, as also practiced at Twycross and Marwell. John Heyworth's considered choice of the name 'Cotswold Wildlife Park' reflected its separation from commercial zoo 'franchises'. It was to be a significant departure from the concrete, urban menageries of earlier decades, with open exhibits situated in beautiful natural surroundings, yet retaining an intimacy unavailable to the new brand of drive-through safari parks. The initial aim was not the exhibition of an existing animal collection, as at Twycross, or the conservation intentions of Marwell, but the preservation of an existing estate through a radical gamble on land diversification. John Heyworth explored the options, recognised the favourable conditions and seized his opportunity in 1969. Ambition and energy, nevertheless, did not necessarily guarantee success, so knowledge and experience were the first qualities he sought with which to transform his vision into reality.

Chapter 2

"A constant battle with the builders"

1969-70

By 1969, John Heyworth was actively exploring the possibility of opening up the grounds and gardens surrounding the Manor House to the public. Despite the increasing popularity of animal collections in Britain at this time, any financial investment in such a transformation was uncertain. The simplest, and most risk-averse, option available was the abandonment and demolition of part, or all, of the Manor House, but this was quickly disregarded. Another route was through collaboration with the Chipperfield safari park franchise, which would convert the open space into a popular attraction. The price of such a partnership, however, was deemed too great, entailing reduced landowner influence, an equal split in profits and winding concrete roads scarring the landscape. John Heyworth's determination to maintain independent control was to be a guiding principle of the Cotswold Wildlife Park from its beginning, preserving the natural beauty of the Manor House site. This required the venture to be completely supported by his private finance and a considerable bank loan. No outside funding or government grants were available to the prospective Park at a time when public coffers were strained. Enquiries were made to the Countryside Commission about a possible 75% reimbursement of car park and road building costs, but a dismissive reply explained it was considered "not appropriate to aid a project which could be said to be commercially viable" and any aid was limited to providing free picnic facilities.[15] Commercial viability was an absolute necessity for John Heyworth, who estimated capital of £40,000 (equivalent to more than £500,000 in 2011) was required to realise his vision. The ultimate decision to embark on the venture, therefore, could be described as an expensive leap in the dark, making it vital to secure the right skills and personalities to ensure success.

John Heyworth's ambition was the most important catalyst for creating the Park. The Park's first curator wrote at the time, "With farming becoming more and more difficult, [he] hopes to make it into an extremely paying proposition."[16] Mr Heyworth held a private estate of 3500 acres, 1500 of which were run by his farm manager, 1600 farmed by tenants and the remainder existing as well-maintained woodlands. A herd of prize-winning Red Poll cattle, among the best in England, was also kept at Bradwell Grove, a passion inherited from his grandfather. They were increasingly unable to compete with Friesian dairy cattle, however, and the sale of the majority of these beloved animals in September 1969 represented Mr Heyworth's increasing commitment to the wildlife park project, regardless of the sacrifices. His personal papers of this time are full of notes, ideas and proposals written in his characteristic tiny scrawl, meticulously organised and stored. Potential business collaborations to save costs were explored, such as seeking discounted plants from various local nurseries in return for favourable advertisement. All his efforts in those early months were channelled into researching the recent national revolution in recreation and planning the transformation of his own estate as efficiently as possible.

John Taylor: a useful ally

Heyworth recognised, moreover, that enthusiasm would not produce results unless it was partnered with expertise. Fortunately, a short article in *Farm and Country* magazine had directed him towards an experienced person who could provide the valuable advice he required. It profiled the efforts made by John Taylor to combine dairy farming alongside tourism at Cricket St Thomas in Somerset through innovative methods of diversification. In conjunction with Major J J Ogilvie, a retired serviceman with wide experience of tropical animals, Taylor had established a wildlife centre on his own estate in 1967. Beginning with a pair of Australian black swans, adopted as its symbol, the collection soon expanded to include varieties of crane, deer, wallabies and waterfowl.[17]

John Taylor had trained at the Royal Agricultural College and qualified as a land agent, and was able to bring fresh ideas and methods to maximise the potential of a traditional estate. Heyworth was intrigued by this story as Cricket St Thomas closely reflected his own intentions, with its focus on birds and smaller animals, and he eagerly made contact in December 1968. The two men found that they got on well and quickly formed a close, productive relationship. On his first visit to Bradwell Grove, Taylor was optimistic about the area's potential, believing if "developed in the right way it could preserve the house and grounds in a state which will provide endless enjoyment to others".[18] He gratefully seized the opportunity to provide his services for three years on a consultancy basis, at a fee of 5% of gross turnover.

In the first few months of 1969, correspondence between Taylor and Heyworth was energetic, as they formulated plans and debated the basic shape of the Park's layout. Unlike Victorian menageries, establishing a zoo was no longer simply a case of collecting numerous animal specimens for exhibition. Many more mundane practical details had to be considered, such as convenient services essential for encouraging public appreciation. As a result, Taylor's initial advice focused on the crucial infrastructure required for accommodating a large number of visitors.[19]

The first concern, for example, was to sow an area of free-draining land with a tough grass mixture to provide a car park. Hard-standing ground was only absolutely necessary to accommodate the heavy coaches, said Taylor, supported by the valuable insight that "the drivers get upset if they get bogged down". Access also had to be improved, with the laying of a ten-foot-wide hardcore road on the existing front drive to ensure an easy flow of vehicles. He recommended expenditure on the exit, however, be kept to a minimum, hoping a new entrance road could quickly be installed past South Lodge, with the drive then operating as the exit. As evidenced by the continuing use of the original exit for over 40 years,

Taylor's advice was gratefully received but not always enacted.

Perhaps the most fortuitous outcome of this relationship was the introduction of Brian Sinfield, the Park's first curator, to the project. John Heyworth had been particularly concerned to find an animal keeper with the vision, dynamism and determination to build the wildlife collection from the ground up. Available people to fulfil these demanding criteria were rare, but fortunately Taylor and Sinfield had first met when Brian was working at Flamingo Park in North Yorkshire, which had acted in an advisory capacity for Cricket St Thomas. It seemed to be an unofficial training ground for zoo curators, with one former head keeper running Thetford Wildlife

Brian Sinfield: curator, 1970-75

Brian was a tall, handsome man with dark hair and a wide knowledge of the zoo world. Since leaving school at 16, he had worked in various zoos in Britain and Australia. He particularly enjoyed working with the gorillas at Taronga Park in Sydney, which he described as "one of the most beautifully situated zoos in the world". At Flamingo Park, he was employed as superintendent/curator, essentially running the whole enterprise. The lack of independence or a serious challenge, however, caused increasing restlessness. He was intrigued by the telegram inviting him to Bradwell Grove and a visit was arranged for Friday 18 April 1969.

When first travelling up the drive with Ann, his partner, Brian was immediately struck by the gothic facade of the Manor House. As he wandered around the grounds with John Heyworth, his excitement increased and his "imagination began to work overtime".[20] The magnificent, old outbuildings could be converted into animal houses and flat, open fields dotted with well-established trees offered ideal paddocks. The nucleus of the Park was to be a three-acre walled area, the old kitchen garden, and the overgrown weeds failed to prevent Brian from visualising the many opportunities the site provided. The key position was quickly offered and eagerly accepted, forming an essential partnership which was to shape the foundation of the Park. Mr Heyworth's assessment of his new curator – "obviously good with animals, although I should not think office work is much in his line"[21] – proved to be an excellent judgement of character, neatly summarising Brian's proactive approach. The day before moving to Burford to take up the new position, Brian had finished a reptile and aquarium display in a huge dome on Hastings pier, ready just in time for its mayoral opening. The same week he had married Ann, leaving no time for a honeymoon.

Park in Norfolk and another becoming manager of Windsor Safari Park. John Heyworth hoped the successful trend would continue with his own venture.

The head gardener

The final indispensable individual involved in establishing the Park was Les Scott, the head gardener. According to Sinfield, he was just as important as the animal department, if not more so, for tending the areas between the enclosures and creating the beautiful aesthetic surrounding the Park which appealed to so many visitors.[22]

After active service in the Second World War, Les married his childhood sweetheart, Lillian, in 1947. He then spent two years learning the gardening trade in the parks department at Weymouth. It was here he developed his skills by producing and tending formal flowerbeds, which were to become an important feature of his work at the Park. The Scotts moved to Oxfordshire in 1949 to tend gardens at Wychwood and Cornbury Park, but their true "big adventure" (as Lillian described it) did not begin until 20 years later.[23] On the recommendation of his friend Michael Hughes-Hallet, the agent at Cornbury Park, John Heyworth sent a letter to Les, seeking his help in transforming his potential wildlife park at Burford. He was "looking for a man who will wish to stay on the estate for the rest of his life... I believe the job has great prospects". Upon viewing the grounds, Les and Lillian had to agree with this assessment, despite having tentatively embarked on an independent landscaping business of their own just a month beforehand. Their decision was finally sealed when Mr Heyworth made the tranquil South Lodge on the estate available to them, which became their beloved home with a lifelong tenancy. Les was to fulfil all the hopes and faith placed in him by his employer right up to his final retirement 30 years later, in 1999.

Before any work could begin, however, planning permission had to be sought from the county council, a potentially daunting battle with local government bureaucracy. John Heyworth had first approached the council in February about a possible change of land use from agricultural to recreational. Plans of the estate were drawn up detailing the position of various attractions, particularly highlighting the central role of the Walled Garden and a children's play area to be situated to the north-west of the Manor House. Disappointment loomed when a neighbouring resident with a prominent position on the council planning board was hostile to the proposed plans. His opposition nearly undermined the entire scheme before it had even begun. Fortunately, however, John Heyworth had formed a close friendship with the long-serving clerk of the council, Gerald Gale Burkitt, during his period as High Sheriff of Oxfordshire in 1962. Burkitt was able to inform Heyworth of a time when the principal objector was on holiday, allowing the wildlife park plans to be submitted as soon as he was away.[24] Permission was consequently granted on 29 July, just 11 days after the final application, stating acceptance of the "use of Walled Garden open to public for display of birds, domestic animals and small wild animals in aviaries and ponds [and the] erection of temporary aviaries and housing for monkeys, etc".[25] Once the green light had been officially given, the hard work started in earnest, with the intention of opening at Easter the following year.

The Walled Garden

As the Walled Garden was to be the central point of interest for the opening season, its transformation was a key priority requiring considerable effort. In its former days as the Manor's kitchen garden, a neat path flanked by apple trees had led up the centre, with other minor paths bordered by box hedges. Les Scott, however, remembered encountering the area for the first time, with "the wrought iron gates at the entrance... chained and padlocked, [having] not been opened for 20 years. The whole area was covered with brambles which were growing over the ten-foot-high perimeter walls".[26] Two retired estate employees, George Pitelen, who had worked as head herdsman for 38 years, and Sid Simpson, formed the rest of the early gardening team. They began the arduous task of clearing weeds, levelling the ground and preparing it for new planting. With little experience aside from their own gardens, Les had to teach them on the job. Three connected glasshouses, to be replaced in time with a Tropical House, had grown carnations, rare hot-house plants, nectarines and peaches. Victorian greenhouses, reputed to be the oldest in Oxfordshire, were sited in the walled annex. Unsurprisingly, these had fallen into disrepair and Lillian

Scott, with her youngest daughter, helped by cleaning out and making them fit for purpose. She remembered the minimal resources available to the gardening team, who were always careful to keep one eye on their limited tools whenever they put them down, unless they were willing for them to disappear to perform another task elsewhere.[27]

The details of the Walled Garden evolved over the summer months of 1969, during many discussions between John Heyworth, Brian Sinfield, Les Scott and John Taylor. No formal, accurately measured plans were created and work mainly followed a rough design drawn by Brian. The idea was to present birds in the largest aviaries possible with animals in walled enclosures. The layout needed to provide a wonderful plant display but also offset and complement these exhibits with green backdrops where necessary. In an early plan, the aviaries and enclosures bordering the walls were followed by a circular path, while a 20-foot-wide fish and water-plant pond was envisioned where two straight paths intersected at the centre of the garden. Ring-tailed lemurs were to be kept in an enclosure surrounded by a small moat in the north-east corner. Smooth otters were to be exhibited in the south-west corner, while penguins were originally intended to be accommodated in an enclosure in the wider grounds. By June, a seal pool was being contemplated and the penguins eventually became the new occupants. Only the hornbills in the north-west corner retained their originally planned spots. The footprint of the Park emerged gradually as various ideas were articulated, considered and dismissed or rejected.

While Mr Heyworth's small staff worked incessantly, the sheer scale of the construction work required a number of building contractors to be employed. Local knowledge of the new venture near Burford had spread like wildfire and many labouring companies were keen to offer their services. The car park and internal roads, by B G Faherty Ltd, were the greatest construction expense, costing £3900 even though gravel on a hard base was selected as a cheaper temporary alternative to tarmac. E Taylor & Son converted two of the Manor House store rooms into public WCs, as well as constructing the red panda pit around the wych elm close to the house and restoring the conservatory to a useable condition. The firm of Stanley W Davis was occupied with renovating the battlements and repairing patches of the kitchen garden wall. For the vast amount of excavation and foundation work necessary, contractors with JCB diggers at a reasonable cost were vital, particularly when electricity and telephone lines, water pipes and drains all had to be extended to service the new offices and animal enclosures. One such person was Peter Pauling, an enterprising local farmer who was most involved in the initial groundwork for the Walled Garden. With his new digger, he hoped to earn enough money to buy the lease on a farm at Chadlington. Due to the sheer amount of labour required at the Park, he was successful in this ambition and the farm remains in the family today.

Public toilets proved to be among the more difficult considerations in establishing the Park. An estimate of the likely number of visitors had to be agreed, then sufficient facilities planned to accommodate them. Brian Sinfield had experienced the problems that arose at other zoos when toilet blocks with inadequate water supply struggled with the volume of use by thousands of visitors on busy summer days. Determined to avoid similar situations, great attention was paid to installing large water pipes to all such facilities. Even such precautions, however, were inadequate to cope with the Park's popularity. One employee remembered how nearly every Sunday, when visitor numbers were at a peak, a hastily compiled team would converge on manholes armed with tools to remove unpleasant blockages.[28] This was just one of the many teething problems John Heyworth, Brian and their staff had to resolve once the enterprise opened to the public.

Despite hurried and haphazard construction in the few months before the Park opened, very few unseen obstacles or disasters hindered the process. Although Brian had complained to his wife that building a zoo had nothing to do with animals and was always a "constant battle between you and the builders", relationships with the contractors were generally productive.[29]

The major exception, which was to cause near-permanent headaches, was the penguin pool in the south-west corner of the Walled Garden. The builder responsible was described as "rugged and loveable", but he was as independent-minded as the curator. Clashes were therefore frequent when he failed to follow detailed instructions, providing his own artistic interpretation for the depth of the pool, the sweep of a wall or the type of concrete finish right for the penguins' feet. The result was so inadequate that an entire facelift was required in the autumn of 1971. The pool depth was reduced to and the enclosure resurfaced with a mixture of white cement and marble chippings. The filtration system was to prove even more difficult, the perfect example of how seeking economies sometimes proved more expensive in the long term. With promises from the contractor of cheap effectiveness, an indiscreet 500-gallon, converted water tank was installed in a purpose-built filter shed. Gravel and sand from the paths were then added as filter media but, unsurprisingly, failed and the working association was terminated on a sour note. On the whole, however, John Heyworth believed the Park established an effective and mutually beneficial relationship with local labour over the years.[30]

There could be no Wildlife Park without the building of animal enclosures, and the star in this field was a Saint Helenian man called Alfred Brooks. He was relatively small, about five feet seven, but tough and "as wiry as a mountain goat".[31] Alf was an indefatigably hard worker and an excellent carpenter. Previously living on the estate with his wife Mildred and their young family, contact had been lost when he had moved to Oxford to establish his own building firm. John Heyworth realised his woodworking capabilities would be invaluable and sent a speculative letter to Alf's mother in October 1969. Fortunately the invitation to return to Bradwell Grove found its way to the intended recipient and was accepted. Alf's small team swiftly became responsible for constructing most of the first aviaries in the Walled Garden and the surrounding area. They were of a simple rectangular design, intended to provide the greatest flight area for the birds. Four-by-two timbers or old telegraph poles, requested from the General Post Office, were used for the uprights and beams across the top. Chain link was used to enclose the larger aviaries, with inch-square weld-mesh used to house smaller birds. In order to prevent light reflection, and allow visitors to view the occupants, the final arduous task was to paint the wire black or green. It was a revelation, therefore, when plastic-coated weld mesh was discovered, saving the valuable man hours needed to get the rest of the Park ready on time.[32] Only the hornbills provided any resistance, twisting the mesh and tearing off the plastic coating, until Perspex sheets were installed to protect the corner targeted by their hostility. Mr Heyworth believed Alf's proficiency and dedication was vital for allowing the Park to keep to schedule and open at Easter 1970.[33]

Acquiring the animals

With a quarantine block and several enclosures completed, it was finally time to acquire the first animals for the Park. In August 1969, it was still general practice for zoos to purchase their wildlife from animal dealers, who regularly issued catalogues of their current stock. More reputable and professional firms, such as Ravensden Zoological Company, kept their stock in better conditions than others, but these were still far from ideal without the care and attention of dedicated keepers. With the lack of collaboration, or even communication, among the British or European zoo communities in the 1960s, however, the dealers were the only option and therefore essential for a fledgling venture such as the Cotswold Wildlife Park. John Heyworth lacked the resources to collect animals from their native countries, like the practice of the Chipperfield enterprise, or the experience to wade through the bureaucracy and red tape required. The price had to be considered within the wider context, as the Park would eventually grow to contribute greatly to education and work with animals across the world.

Mr Heyworth's original hope had been to focus on exhibiting birds, particularly ornamental waterfowl. One pair of diamond doves, two pairs of green glossy starlings and three pairs of grey Java sparrows were among the first orders placed. Such displays, however, were not considered exciting enough by the general British public. In order to fulfil their expectations and draw sufficient crowds to sustain the business, the acquisition of more exotic animals was required. Heyworth and Sinfield, however, were determined to keep the satisfaction of popular interest within the means and intended ethos of the Park. Lions, giraffes, elephants and the higher primates were ignored, as the resources were simply not available to provide satisfactory enclosures. In a letter to John Taylor, Heyworth wrote, "I think we must limit the livestock for 1970 to numbers that can be looked after with local help rather than employ a full-time man, but hope that big expansion will then be justified."[34] With these needs and restrictions in mind, the main body of original stock had been agreed by the end of August. The order was to include a pair of red pandas, five Bennett's wallabies, two pairs of coatis, six prairie dogs, two pairs of smooth otters, four common seals, a pair of squirrel monkeys, two pairs of capuchin monkeys, a dozen chipmunks, two porcupines, two llamas, four Humboldt penguins and six Chilean flamingos, among a variety of other bird species, totalling £4219, 12 shillings and 4 pence.

Any remaining illusions Mr Heyworth may have held about the ease of managing a wildlife park were quickly dispelled by the appearance of the animals themselves. The wallabies were the first to arrive, on 20 August 1969, after an advertisement offering a group of five had been spotted in a newspaper. Brian Sinfield had to make the long journey to Lancashire, where the marsupials were kept privately. Finding the animals penned up in a corner of a field, and informed they were relatively tame, the curator hoped catching them would be an easy task. Unfortunately this did not prove to be the case and the wallabies refused to be taken quietly. After an energetic hour, however, they were all placed in wooden crates, ready for the journey to their new home. Temporarily housed in the eastern annex of the Walled Garden, still overgrown with grass and weeds, they were joined by a pair of sarus crane a few days later, which arrived so late in the evening that they had to be pinioned by torchlight. From that point, a constant flow of animals arrived and the number of species at Cotswold Wildlife Park has had an upwards trajectory ever since.[35]

The dangers of animal keeping were also quickly realised, with the lives of John Heyworth and Brian Sinfield seriously threatened months before the Park was due to open. The menace did not arise from an escaped angry carnivore or a poisonous reptile carelessly handled, but a seemingly innocuous parrot. With several smaller aviaries prepared in the area of the Walled Garden designated as Pets' Corner, John and Brian decided to take a trip in September to choose some birds from an animal dealer.[36] One pair of white-faced tree ducks and some African grey parrots were purchased, among others. With the birds placed on the back seat of the car, the two men returned to the Park, keeping the windows closed to protect against particularly cold weather. They thought little of the poor ventilation in the vehicle until they were both struck by flu-like symptoms, including soaring temperatures reaching 40 °C. Doctors considered and debated, specialists were consulted and even officials at the Ministry of Health were informed. Finally, the disease was correctly diagnosed as psittacosis, caused by a bacterium carried by many birds, and heavy doses of antibiotics were prescribed. Confined to their beds for several weeks while their families fretted over their health, the two recovering men were mainly concerned by this inconvenient delay to their plans.[37]

Despite the lack of large, well-known animals at the beginning, one species was intended to be a somewhat unusual attraction, allowing the Park to stand out. The red panda is an arboreal mammal, looking not dissimilar to a rusty raccoon, with thick red fur and white patched face. Considerably smaller and less famous than their black and white cousins, they live in the high forests of western China and the eastern Himalayas, at an altitude of 7000 to 12000 feet. They also survive well in captivity and it was decided that they had the potential for great popular appeal. Due to its charm and relative rarity in zoos, the red panda was chosen as the Park's widely publicised first emblem. It appeared on letterheads, advertising material, the entrance display and key signs on the main road. This was very successful and Brian Sinfield was pleased with the number of people talking about the new wildlife park and its pandas. A walled enclosure was built around a tree close to the Manor House, with a large barrel installed in its branches as sleeping quarters.

A fundamental error, however, lay in the failure to acquire these figurehead animals. On 6 March 1970, the Government had announced a ban on the importation of domestic pets, fearing the spread of rabies to Britain after a virulent outbreak in Europe. This was to include all animals related to cats, dogs and rodents but the cute creatures from China appeared to escape the legislation. However, hopes were shattered when news from the Ministry of Agriculture informed the Park that red pandas had also been placed on the rabies list and were therefore prohibited from entering the country. Brian began calling his contacts in the animal trade with a rising state of panic, only to be told what he needed was available but stuck on the wrong side of the English Channel. Permission for special importation was impossible and no pandas were forthcoming from another domestic zoo. Days before opening, Barry Pape, an animal dealer friend of Brian's, suggested a pair of African civet cats could act as a suitable replacement. They were a similar size and shape to the red pandas, but grey with black stripes and patches. Although they could only pass as the originally intended animal by someone squinting in poor light, they were nevertheless interesting in their own right and were consequently purchased and installed in the enclosure. An embarrassed note enclosed in the guidebook regretted the absence of the red pandas but their 'understudies' proved popular on their rare appearances (being largely nocturnal). The pandas themselves did not arrive to compete for the public's attention until July 1972.[38]

With only weeks to go until opening day, the Park was a flurry of frantic activity and everyone feared that preparations would not be finished in time. Teams of handymen with a previously nonchalant approach to labour were suddenly redoubling their efforts. Alf's work remained dedicated, dividing his toil between erecting a refreshment kiosk against the side of the Walled Garden and constructing a giant vulture aviary close to it. Brian thought Mr Heyworth, although "characteristically reserved", must have been secretly panicking, while he personally was in a "terrible state" of stress and anticipation.[39] Les Scott's team had dedicated all their efforts to the space and enclosures within the Walled Garden, making it attractive and presentable in a remarkably short amount of time, but had been unable to make a huge impact on the wider grounds. Rooms in the Manor House had been converted to provide important amenities for the public, changing drastically from their original use. A small gift shop, managed by Ann Sinfield, occupied the dining room, with colourful toys packing the shelves. Tables and chairs for restaurant diners had been installed in the drawing room and conservatory. The food servery was to be found in the old library while the adjoining billiards room now housed the kitchen facilities. The billiards table had been removed to fulfil new duties in the penguin pool, acting as the foundation for a landscaped waterfall. Other areas, such as the otter pond and the lake enclosure, however, remained far from complete.

Journalists visiting during a press day on 18 March 1970, nine days before opening, found an area hugely transformed, with much to admire, but still some distance from perfection. John Heyworth had achieved his intention of introducing wildlife in aesthetically pleasing, natural enclosures, with views largely unhindered by fences or caging. His investment had been substantial, with £29,907 spent up to 28 February 1970, mostly on construction and purchasing the animals. Small tidying jobs remained to be finished around the place, such as the removal of an old chandelier from above the food counter in the Manor House, the planting of the civet enclosure and the covering of a well in the Walled Garden. The garden paths remained muddy tracks, awaiting their gravel surface which would otherwise be disrupted by busy construction work. The members of the media, however, were suitably satisfied and delivered positive verdicts. All those involved in the creation of the Wildlife Park now nervously awaited the judgement of the general public, as they were to be let through the gates for the first time.

Chapter 3

"Call this a wildlife park?"

1970-74

The Cotswold Wildlife Park opened to the public for the first time on Good Friday, 27 March 1970. Reflecting 40 years later on how he felt the evening before, John Heyworth believed he hadn't been particularly worried, pausing slightly before adding, "I should have been."[40] The final preparations had been desperate, many areas only just completed, and there was no way of knowing if a year's worth of toil would bring any success. The animals were determined to be as uncooperative as possible for the big day. A mound of earth in the prairie dog enclosure had been freshly turfed the previous day but, during the night, this had been rolled up again as the animals foraged for food, undermining a previously pleasing visual display.[41] After resolving last minute issues of this kind, Brian Sinfield walked up the long drive to open the gates at 10am, with a mixture of fear and anticipation. He was hugely relieved to find that word about the Park had spread and a number of cars were awaiting entry, full of curious families eager to make the most of the rare fine weather in an outdoor attraction. Without any special commemoration or fanfare, they were welcomed in – and that's when problems began to escalate.

In retrospect, Mr Heyworth decided opening for the busy Easter weekend, while good for publicity and income, was not one of his more sensible ideas. His small staff was enthusiastic but inexperienced, overwhelmed by the huge crowds flooding into the Park. Everyone available to help was called up for duty, including office staff, estate workers and family members. The ticket machines at the paybox struggled to cope and promptly jammed, causing delays and frustration. Animal keepers were drafted in as emergency ticket sellers, their pockets quickly brimming with loose change, yet the queue of the vehicles continued to lengthen. The goodwill of local communities, largely encouraging and interested in the new attraction on their doorstep, was severely tested as the traffic jam snaked up the A361 and beyond the Burford roundabout over two miles away. Once in the Park, the many visitors were able to enjoy their beautiful surroundings and appreciate the dedication invested in the exhibits. The public amenities, however, were not adequate for such an unexpected number of people, many clamouring for refreshments which created the inevitable need to use the already strained lavatory system. Most of the toilets either ran short of water or blocked up. By the time the last visitor left, the staff collapsed, completely exhausted, only to repeat the whole saga the next day.

Such an overwhelming response was nevertheless considerably more welcome than a Park devoid of paying customers. Around 17,000 people entered during the four-day Easter weekend, at 5 shillings (25p) for an adult and 2 shillings (10p) for a child, making £2648 at the gate and providing an encouraging start for the season. An unimpressive April, taking just £1516 from ticket sales, caused a few worried frowns but these were swiftly wiped away with May's figures. Around 73,000 people had visited by the end of that month, with £8200 earned on the gate and a corresponding rise in retail profits. Mr Heyworth had calculated that a minimum annual attendance of 100,000 was required to cover costs before any capital was available for expansion, so these figures provided optimism for a thriving future. The Wildlife Park was already earning a small but solid reputation for beautiful and well-maintained grounds, as it aimed from the beginning "to present animals in conditions as near to those found in their natural environment as possible".[42]

So what did these first visitors encounter? The red-bricked Walled Garden was the nucleus of the Park, enclosing a diverse range of animals, birds and plants in a flat, open space. The south-west corner housed the troublesome penguin pool, which Humboldt penguins shared with common seals and a white pelican. Visitors were able to get so close that, towards the end of the first season, one unfortunate boy found his head in the pelican's mouth and it was then thought expedient to install a light fence to keep the birds away from the wall.[43] The small mammal enclosure nearest to the pool housed the destructive prairie dogs. A neatly rounded lawn along the south wall, bordered by bedding plants tended by Les Scott and with a pond at its centre, accommodated six Chilean flamingos and a variety of ornamental ducks.

On opening day, the pond enclosure held just two JCB diggers clearing sludge from its bottom; it would be several months before additional flamingos and waterfowl could be found there. In the south-east corner of the Walled Garden, a pair of smooth otters gambolled in their landscaped sloping enclosure, which included a large tank and viewing screen through which they could be seen swimming underwater. A grass mound enclosure for the coatis, surrounded by a stone retaining wall and a concrete ditch, completed the exhibits in the southern side of the Walled Garden.

The aviaries, Alf's handiwork, were just as impressive. Great and pied hornbills, toucans, Reeve's pheasants and rare black storks could all be found in the north-west corner. When Brian had been explaining his vision for this corner to Mr Heyworth, the owner had gently enquired whether hornbills ate other birds and, once assured that they did not, suggested that a mixture of different sized birds could be kept together.[44]

This created a more attractive and interesting display. The mixing of species, although requiring considerable trial and error, luck and constant monitoring, became an important aspect of the Park's exhibits. The largest aviary occupied the north-east corner and stood 100 feet long, 20 feet wide and 12 feet high. A pool was created with cement and the remaining area landscaped with sand banks, huge rocks and dead oak boughs. It held scarlet and sacred ibis, tiger bittern, grey and great blue heron, wood stork and European spoonbill. Two remaining aviaries stood in the middle of the garden, alongside the gravel paths which wound around gnarled apple trees, pristine lawns and vibrant flowerbeds. One contained purple glossy starlings, pagoda mynahs, greater Indian hill mynahs and white-crested laughing thrushes; the other had parakeets, pheasants and mousebirds. Finally, in the middle of the north wall, the old conservatory held six vivaria among the plants to contain cold-blooded animals, including an Indian python, a boa constrictor and chameleons. It thus served as the first Reptile House, albeit makeshift and very temporary.

Close to the greenhouses and potting shed adjoining the main Walled Garden, Pets' Corner contained a number of domestic animals. A fenced yard contained a grey donkey, lambs and several goats, while rustic wooden hutches full of rabbits, guinea pigs and chinchillas lined the walls. Children were encouraged to mix freely and interact with them. This was clearly a very popular area and "reached saturation point in a very short time with so many people confined within its walls".[45] As a result, it was extended for the 1971 season to include parrots and parakeets. Uncle Mac, the tame blue and yellow macaw, proved to be a favourite, along with Buster the toucan, who was too aggressive to be kept with the other birds. A pen for a pair of porcupines was also built, which had to be lined with concrete to prevent them from digging an escape. For many schoolchildren from towns and cities, Pets' Corner provided a rare opportunity to get close to and touch animals, making it a memorable part of their visit.

At this point, exhibits in the wider grounds of the Park were sparse. A llama pen lay between the main car park and the Manor House, where the shaggy South American pack animal grazed alongside the Bennett's wallabies, rheas and a pair of elegant sarus cranes. A single aviary for birds of prey stood alongside the path leading from the Walled Garden to the adventure playground, but its only inhabitants were one pair each of bateleur and tawny eagles. Demoiselle, crowned and Lilford's cranes roamed at will in the walkthrough area around the lake. Mr Heyworth had originally considered installing gibbons on the island at its centre but it was eventually decided that the practicalities of making an enclosure escape-proof were too great, and the idea was dropped. The African civets, 'squatting' in the red panda enclosure, were the last exhibit of individual note. In total, the Park could boast 12 mammal species, 62 bird species and 20 species of reptiles and amphibians, with ambitious plans for expansion.

The collection grows

Improvements, moreover, could not halt even though the Park was now open to visitors and work had to continue throughout the busy summer months as the animal collection grew. The otter pool was finally completed: in June, builders began to convert an old stable towards the rear of the Manor into a permanent house for a pair of pumas.[46] After removing the tin roof and blocking the chimney, two remotely controlled metal traps were installed to give access to a large pen, made of a heavy timber framework and weld mesh cage front. The new accommodation proved to satisfy the felines so much that they were among the first mammals to breed at the Park, in October 1971, and their frequent litters soon began to cause problems when new homes for the cubs could not be found.

August saw the focus of attention shift to the hitherto neglected lake area. A pair of secretary birds was purchased and kept in a grass paddock separated from the main walkthrough with further fencing. Nearby, Freddy the Brazilian tapir had quickly settled into his wooded grass enclosure after arriving from Dublin Zoo. He was joined by a female, Tippy, loaned by Victor Manton at Whipsnade Zoo, where her ancient quarters were being demolished with no plans to replace them. As an experiment, a path for the public ran through the centre of this pen, bordered only by a single wooden rail through which the tapirs could pass from one side to the other. The friendly animals stood almost permanently by the gate, awaiting attention from their visitors. Unfortunately, they only succeeded in frightening their naive audience and prevented them from entering. The tapirs were also masterful escape artists, finding their huge bulk could weaken the main perimeter fence. They were frequently discovered munching beech leaves or oak saplings guiltily in nearby woods.[47] In the end, they had to be confined to one side of the path, with an additional inner fence built and the existing perimeter strengthened. Five adjutant storks from India, standing five feet tall with huge beaks, were also kept in this improved enclosure.

Following these gradual improvements throughout the season, the management felt willing to apply for membership of the Federation of Zoological Gardens of Great Britain and Ireland. This had been established by zoo owners in 1967, recognising a need to self-regulate their collections and promote the raising of standards. Its original members feared that commercial newcomers to the industry, such as the Chipperfield enterprises and Scotia Investments, would harm their reputations. The Federation was intended not as a trade association but to work for the benefit of wild animals in captivity. It became the leading organisation for the improvement of zoo ethics, and John Knowles, founder of Marwell, particularly stressed the importance of discussion and collaboration encouraged by meetings of the Federation's council and committees.[48]

Knowles was aware of its limitations, recognising that reliance on membership income meant collections of a wide range of standards could be found under its umbrella. Inspections carried out by fellow Federation members, however, were better than no regulation at all and the subsequent reports contained valuable constructive criticism. The first inspection at Cotswold Wildlife Park was carried out on 23 September 1970. The inspectors were "very impressed by the attractive layout of the gardens and grounds and the high standard of tidiness maintained". The design of the aviaries and high quality of their construction were also highly commended. Improvements were suggested for safety around the puma enclosure and the hygiene of food preparation. Overall, though, the Park received glowing praise for its early efforts and became a full member in November 1970.

John Heyworth and his employees could be pleased about a great deal, therefore, when the first season came to a close at the end of October. Over 200,000 people had passed through the gates, surpassing all initial estimations. A diverse and interesting collection of animal species had been gathered and settled, while early teething problems with the public were gradually being resolved. Most importantly, the investment in spacious, well-maintained animal housing had been praised as an example of good management, which ensured the stock was healthier and lived longer. Complacency could not be allowed, however, and everyone realised more improvements had to be made. In his consulting position, John Taylor marvelled at the transformation of the Bradwell Grove estate but gave plenty of advice for future changes. The path from the Walled Garden to the adventure playground was considered bare, and he suggested wolves, monkeys or peccaries be installed in enclosures which took advantage of the wooded surroundings. He was particularly insightful about the poor takings from the gift shop and restaurant, which did not reflect a suitable return from the potential custom available to them. As the Walled Garden was the central attraction, he reasoned, not enough visitors were making their way to the Manor House to take advantage of those facilities. More exhibits would have to be introduced to that area in the near future to encourage their use.[49] Finally, it was realised that more headline animal attractions would need to be introduced to please the visitors. In the first months, Mr Heyworth was eager to hear people's opinions of his Park as they got into their cars to leave. On one memorable occasion, a gentleman with his mouth set in a firm line turned to him and replied, "Call this a wildlife park? It's got no bloody animals in it." The harsh words left Heyworth feeling crushed, reluctant to continue his spontaneous surveys, but determined to expand his collection still further.

The reptile collection and aquarium

From that point, a relentless drive to improve on the existing foundations characterised the early years of the Wildlife Park. The reptile collection was deemed the first project worthy of attention in the winter of 1970. For the first season, a small number of animals had been kept in the old conservatory in the Walled Garden, which was divided into three sections. The first contained young Mississippi alligators and spectacled caimans in a heated pool, with a dry land area of sand and gravel. The middle section was reserved for tropical plants and a number of small birds, including yellow-winged sugarbirds, Indian white eyes and orange-gorgeted flycatchers. The third section held a series of glass-fronted, plywood cabinets for 17 species of snake, lizard, tortoise and amphibian. At a time without many health and safety regulations, these were serviced from the public area at the front, and no space was available for off-show animal husbandry.[50] An outdoor circular 'reptilium' stood in front of the conservatory, where a concrete wall surrounded a central grassy mound and pond for North American and diced water snakes. This accommodation was adequate but always considered temporary and the guidebook noted the reptiles would be moved to "more spacious and permanent quarters" as their numbers grew.

Preparations for a replacement had been under way since

catastrophe had struck just before opening day. During a freezing night, a power failure had caused all the electric heating to be cut off. Without a backup generator and well-insulated cages, the reptile keeper was dismayed the following morning to discover his charges extremely cold and close to death, in an advanced state of torpor. A rescue team was hastily assembled by Brian Sinfield, who helped wrap the perilously sick animals in pillowcases and place them on hot water bottles. They were then transported across the Park to his flat in the Manor House, causing a bit of a surprise for his wife. The scaly guests were placed in a warm bath, heads tenderly held above the surface, to regain more of their body heat. For the next 24 hours, boa constrictors in blankets were warmed by the fire and green iguanas recovered resting on the radiators. Through this prompt action, the lives of most of the collection were saved and a costly crisis averted. The most significant casualty was a rare crocodilian, which had only just been brought to the Wildlife Park for safe-keeping while its owner went on holiday. Unfortunately, this near priceless animal died while the Park's own alligators made a full recovery.[51]

In the winter of 1970, therefore, lessons were learned from this experience as work began on converting the stable block at the rear of the Manor into the new Reptile House. When starting the Park, John Heyworth had been keen to ensure changes did not detract from the original setting. The old building, therefore, was an ideal site. At the rear, a dividing wall between four stables was demolished, creating space for the new crocodile enclosure. Water was heated by an immersion system before flowing over a waterfall into the pool and circulating back again. A wire mesh framework on the walls was plastered with coloured cement to provide a natural rock effect. The limitations of the display's aesthetics were exposed, however, when the vegetation painstakingly planted quickly withered and died. Bricks and mortar, with good heat-retaining properties, were used in the construction of substantial, purpose-built vivaria for the rest of the building. These were fitted with cutting-edge technology: double-glazing for insulation and ultraviolet radiation lamps. An oil-fired heating system, powered by a large boiler in a dusty corner room of the building, was devised by Brian Sinfield, avoiding the danger of future power cuts. The space behind the public exhibits became wholly dedicated to reptile keeping only gradually.[52] Animal husbandry remained, in the words of one former reptile keeper, "off-the-cuff", but the quality of the new Reptile House could be seen by the public as soon as it opened at Easter 1971. The high standard of its collection, and dedication of its staff, quickly secured a well-earned reputation among professionals.[53]

In addition to the main reptile building, an aquarium was built in the adjacent stable block. Experimental fish tanks had been trialled in the conservatory without much success, as the amount of sunlight caused an overwhelming growth of green algae. The inspiration for a renewed attempt came from an unexpected source: a fencing sub-contractor and tropical fish enthusiast called Colin Lord. Hours spent discussing tanks and filters with Brian Sinfield resulted in the opportunity to establish a marine display at the Park. Previously, such exhibits had required the costly transportation of ocean water from the coast, limiting them to the larger established zoos, such as London and Manchester. The practicalities, however, had been made much simpler by the invention of artificial 'sea-salt', with the requisite minerals to be added to fresh water. Lord installed several large glass tanks, which were staggered throughout the aquarium to enable viewing from the sides as well as the front. Decorated with sand and bleached coral, and illuminated with blue fluorescent lighting, the exhibit was ready for its inhabitants.

It finally opened after Easter, behind schedule, and a spectacular variety of fish soon began to arrive. The exotic lionfish, displaying a mane of long poisonous spines along its body and fins, particularly entranced visitors, always attracted to the dangerous and deadly. Orange and white striped clownfish also entertained the public, long before *Finding Nemo*. Critics who felt fish lacked character were disproved by Charlie, the dog-faced pufferfish, who would tamely eat food out of the keeper's hand and rarely performed his defensive inflation act. Freshwater fish were not ignored in the collection and proved interesting in their own right, particularly a shoal of piranhas, with their razor-sharp teeth and ferocious reputation.[54]

Despite the relative ease of set-up, tropical marine fish were temperamental and required constant attention, meaning the history of the Park's aquarium was one of variable success. Feeding required a rigid, complicated schedule, with any leftovers quickly removed to prevent pollution of the tank. This was not simply a case of sprinkling some goldfish flakes on the surface. Daily temperature readings checked the water stayed around 24 °C, while the pH value was to remain around 8, slightly alkaline. A simple undergravel filtration system kept the water clean for as long as possible to keep the occupants healthy, aided in each tank by a cleaner wrasse, a small slim fish which fed upon harmful micro-organisms taken from its larger neighbours' mouths and gills. Once the environment of a tank had become settled, further maintenance was fairly simple, unless disturbed by external interference. The limited space of the aquarium unfortunately meant not enough distance could be maintained between tanks and visitors. Children banging on the glass hoping to stimulate greater activity had an adverse effect on the delicate fish, with several valuable specimens succumbing to stress. A dedicated aquarist called John May had replaced Lord by 1972 but, upon his departure, the general running of the aquarium was taken over by the reptile keepers. By 2000, it was looking unspectacular and tired, whereupon it was converted to house the siamang gibbons and more vivaria for the larger snakes.

Improving the grounds

Returning to 1971, the relocation of the reptiles provided new opportunities for the conservatory site in the Walled Garden. Plans were afoot to replace this large lean-to greenhouse with a new Tropical House, providing the perfect environment in which large, exotic plants could flourish. Work by building contractors began in September, with the roof raised and reglazed, while an efficient system of steam pipe heating with a modern oil-fired boiler provided the essential tropical environment. The partitions that had created three sections were removed, allowing a large open space for landscaping. Les Scott, head gardener, eagerly stepped up to the challenge, artistically constructing various pools and a waterfall at the far end, using about 30 trailer loads of earth and roughly the same amount of large boulders.[55] An enclosure for a pair of rhinoceros iguanas, which had not taken to the dry atmosphere of the Reptile House, was constructed and given a rocky landscape at the opposite end.

Obtaining the necessary flora to fill the building and transport visitors to a tropical jungle was the main problem encountered during this project. The Royal Horticultural Society willingly advised on appropriate plants but it proved difficult to purchase the mature specimens required. Scott and Sinfield speculatively contacted a number of organisations, including Kew and Oxford Botanic Gardens, requesting any surplus large tropical plants, particularly palms. All they received were apologetic letters containing sentiments similar to that of Paignton Zoo's head gardener, who doubted that there was "anyone in this country who would help". The original *bougainvillea* and *plumbago capensis*, which had survived their exposure to the cold weather during the renovation, and since flourished, therefore provided most of the early plant cover. Many other varieties had to be grown from cuttings or young plants, but *dracaena*, *hibiscus*, *colocasia*, rubber plants, banana trees, bamboo and others became well-established through the hard work of the gardening team. On 18 March 1972, five South American hummingbirds were the first to be introduced to their new environment and soon visitors were able to walk among a number of small birds flitting above their heads: white-eyes; sunbirds direct from East Africa with brilliantly coloured plumage; and hoopoes with curved beaks and an orange crest of head feathers. On fine days, the birds had access to an outside flight annex through a sliding hatch in the wall. Mishaps were not entirely avoided, such as the escape within two weeks of three African bee-eaters chasing insects through visitors' legs. Aside from these small problems, however, the Tropical House was an immediate popular success.

Despite the huge investment of time required for this project, continuous gardening improvements were made as Les Scott and his team also turned their attention to the wider grounds. Three mild, wet winters in succession had ensured much of the landscaping work could be done during the Park's closed season. The potting shed was also always bustling at this time, with soils prepared for the seed sowing which commenced in the first week of January. The list of gardening projects was always closely linked to the arrival of new animals, as the team busied themselves with integrating newly constructed aviaries and enclosures with the natural surroundings. Shrubs, including royal purple *buddleia*, *berberis* and *cytisus*, were planted around the spider monkey cage at the rear of the aquarium in spring 1971, while one large bed in the new birds of prey area was dedicated to varieties of *hypericums*. Providing foliage to enhance the animal enclosures provided an interesting set of challenges for Les, who needed to ensure the plants would not be detrimental to the animals' health and would survive their destructive tendencies. Not all inhabitants were appreciative of his efforts. A source of continuing bafflement was the failure of plants to bloom in the otherwise spectacular Tropical House. Blaming temperature fluctuations for a time, the true cause was not found until a pair of fairy blue birds was observed pecking buds off as fast as they could, seemingly for pleasure.[56] The culprits were quickly removed and the plants were able to bloom unmolested.

Increasing amounts of capital were invested in further expansion for the Park, as larger animals arrived to supplement the collection. A young pair of Ankole cattle, domesticated for centuries in East Africa and distinguished by large conical horns, was received from Whipsnade Park. Strong fencing was installed to form a paddock bordering the entrance drive, where they were kept from 1971 along with a flock of donated Jacob's sheep. Of even greater consequence, moreover, were John Heyworth's plans for an African Plains enclosure on the fields in front of the Manor House, where the remaining Red Poll cattle continued to graze. In November 1970, the Sinfields had taken a safari holiday in Kenya, where Brian excitedly reported news about potential animal imports to his boss back in England. Long-term planning was vital, as hoofed animals were likely to be scarce and a year's quarantine under strict conditions was required upon their arrival in Britain.

The African Plains

Conveniently forgetting the original council permission remit for exhibiting "small mammals', the idea was to extend an existing ha-ha, a ditch used in agriculture, to form a mixed paddock of African grazing animals without solid fences despoiling the open view. Carl Hagenbeck had first developed the idea of keeping wild animals behind invisible ditches at his revolutionary zoo at Stellingen, Hamburg, in 1907. He constructed vast panoramas with deep ditches between exhibits. This meant visitors could view an 'African' veldt with lions sunning themselves on rocks in the foreground, gazelles in the middle distance and elephants beyond them. Although separated by the ditches, it gave the impression that the animals all lived together in the same area.

Hagenbeck's work, therefore, inspired the African Plains exhibit at Cotswold Wildlife Park. Ha-has had been used on country estates like Bradwell Grove for centuries, in order to prevent cattle from straying too close to the house or gardens. A planning application was first submitted in October 1971, but members of the board were more than a little concerned about the possibility of wild animals being kept behind what they envisioned as a mere trench. Once reassured that a 1.4m-high retaining wall would be sunk into the ground, with an iron wire fence reaching into the four acre paddock at a 45° angle, the countryside sub-committee finally agreed to the plans in December.

The iconic image of white rhinoceroses grazing sedately in front of a 19th century English manor house, apparently unenclosed, was thus made possible. The most important advantage of the ha-ha was its versatility as a barrier to a number of species of varying sizes. Thomson's gazelles, Grevy zebras, ostriches and rhinos were all housed in the new paddock and generally mixed well, although a famous tabloid photograph of a braying zebra chasing a rhino suggests otherwise. As a precaution, several long, low earth mounds were built to act as escape routes for the animals if conflict arose between them. This would allow the smaller, more manoeuvrable creatures to dodge any hostile attention.

At the Plains' end furthest from the Manor House, a wooden building comprised seven loose boxes to house the hoofed animals. On the opposite side, a solid rhino house was constructed of brick and concrete, with two bays and a public viewing area. Brian Sinfield had visited Chester Zoo and sketched their building on the back of a cigar packet. Returning to the Park, he showed Alf the drawing and asked if he could build it. The answer, of course, was yes. A corrugated fibreglass roof was installed to facilitate once again a blend of wildlife and horticulture, so plants, including *fuchsias*, *magnolia grandiflora* and *fatsia japonica* could be grown, out of reach of the rhinos. Large telegraph poles were set in concrete, with thick steel hawsers running through them to create a hard-standing yard. With construction complete, all that was required were the paddock's new occupants. The zebras were the first to be introduced to their yards in March 1972, followed by the Thomson's gazelles, which had spent a year's quarantine at Bellevue Zoo in Manchester.

The arrival of the white rhinos was eagerly anticipated in the summer. As the second largest land animal after the elephant, they were to be the biggest attraction at the Park by far. It is believed that the name is not derived from their colour but a corruption of the Dutch word *wijd*, meaning 'wide', in reference to the width of the rhinoceros' mouth. With these animals previously near extinction in the 1890s, the efforts of the Natal Parks Board in South Africa ensured a gradual population increase by the 1950s and 1960s. It was arranged for a pair, around five years old, to be brought from there to the Park, at a cost of over £2000 each. The hope was to participate eventually in a conservation scheme to breed the rare species in captivity. For this purpose, groups were sent to San Diego Zoo and Windsor Safari Park at the same time.

Partly motivated by thoughts of publicity, Brian Sinfield had sought to enlist the Royal Air Force for the transportation of these heavy animals. He contacted the camp commander at RAF Brize Norton, the local air base. After receiving confident verbal confirmation over the telephone, the curator cancelled their originally planned passage by ship, only to be told three days later that the arranged flight had been blocked by higher powers. Cursing his luck and desperate to receive the high profile and commercially important animals before the end of the summer tourist season, transportation by sea was once again arranged with great difficulty. After the resulting delay of six weeks, the animals finally arrived in August, lowered in substantial crates by crane. Once released, the bull, Somtuli, caused concern by choosing an unconventional route into his enclosure, charging into the yard fence and ripping the steel hawsers out of the ground, forcing a concrete replacement to be built.[57] After this near-disaster, however, he and his mate, Lebombo, settled right into their new home, where they spent many happy years delighting visitors.

On a smaller scale, other animal additions included European badgers and African leopards, emphasising the range of animals from a number of different sources. An enclosure was built for the badgers in the wooded area close to the bird of prey aviaries. Seventy yards in circumference, this included a small building with glass panels through which the animals could be seen in their underground setts. Artificial tunnels provided an entrance among the roots of tree stumps added to the pen. The badgers had been brought to the Park as orphans and hand-reared. They thus lost their fear of humans but, rather than becoming tame, they became ferocious enemies of many keepers. One of the most dreaded jobs was facing these vicious and territorial animals to clean out the enclosure, which was rebuilt in 1979 to make the task less dangerous.

On the other side of the Park, a leopard cage made from larch poles and wire mesh was constructed behind the zebra house. At first, the cats stayed predominantly among the platforms of the trees incorporated into their enclosure but gradually came to prowl the extra space provided for them and the quality of their housing contributed to their popularity with visitors. This was the first project in an area for planned future development, with a refreshment kiosk and a trio of Bactrian camels from Russia added in 1974, after their year's quarantine spent at Coventry Zoo.

Staffing and catering facilities

Aside from the more newsworthy wildlife expansion at the Park, changes were also made to the amenities and infrastructure. The main expenditure in the early months of 1973, for example, was the tarmacking of the dusty car park and paths in the Walled Garden; such changes were essential for improving the visitor experience.

With the rise in the number of animals, exhibits and amount of space, there was an obvious need to increase the staff. A collection of people as eclectic as the animals, therefore, could be found at the Cotswold Wildlife Park. In 1970, the animal team could be considered small by zoo standards, with just the curator and four full-time keepers, while another two part-time keepers worked at weekends. Richard Pickles and Nick Styles were among the first men hired to care for the animals. In addition, a proud and particular woman called Sheila Curry proved to be an excellent head bird keeper. In the very early days, two young schoolboys, Gerry and Will Manley, joined the staff. They spent all of their spare time working at the Park, getting stuck into the dirtiest of jobs. Brian thought they were "truly remarkable" but the brothers simply enjoyed every minute of their time at the Park.[58]

There was no strict job definition or designated duties for each staff member at this point, however, with everyone helping out where required. Sheila, therefore, also assisted Brian Sinfield in the Reptile House, until the first dedicated reptile keeper, John Coborn, arrived at the beginning of 1972. She left the Park in March 1973, along with Pickles, to take an expedition to Rhodesia. By this point, the reputation of the Park had been established and it was attracting interest from people with impressive work experience. Ken Lock, having worked at London Zoo for several years, arrived to take charge of the mammals, while Richard Martin replaced Sheila on birds. Several big names in the UK zoo world, such as John Coborn and John Simmons, quickly became established and well-respected at the Park in these early years.[59]

For the British public, connoisseurs of the pot of tea and ploughman's sandwich, the catering facilities were an important part of any day out, as well as being some of the most difficult to get right. The Park's early struggles with catering concessionaires well illustrate this point. The first restaurant had a servery in the old library of the Manor House, with patrons dining in the conservatory and drawing room. The kitchen was run by Don Ray, who had originally offered to provide advice and assistance on a commission basis so the Park could set up its own restaurant service. John Heyworth, with so much already on his plate, decided the task was too great and suggested Ray took the lease of the catering facilities for a year at a rent of £650, after the Park had installed all the necessary equipment.

The first season was adequate but Ray was reluctant to entertain plans for catering expansion. After seeking advice from John Taylor, Heyworth ended the association in November 1972 and entered a more ambitious agreement with Mayfield Catering, initially for five years. Customers proved difficult to please as both companies struggled to overcome teething problems, with complaints of high prices and poor service causing Mr Heyworth considerable concern for their poor reflection on his Park. Nevertheless, plans for a cafeteria extension on the west side of the house, overlooking the adventure playground lawn, could be set in motion with the new concessionaire.

This possibility had been investigated as early as April 1970, with space for up to 250 diners planned, including a heated corner enclosure for small alligators and tropical birds. Work began in earnest towards the end of the 1973 summer season but the new building was not finally completed and fully functional until the middle of 1974.

Global recession

The long, frustrating delay in the construction of the cafeteria was not the result of lazy builders, but a global political crisis and national economic problems. In October 1973, a number of Arab Middle Eastern countries had proclaimed an oil embargo in protest against the United States' decision to re-supply the Israeli military during the Yom Kippur War. Oil output was severely reduced and prices rocketed. As a result, plastic production had been cut back and the implication for the Park was the lack of the heavy Perspex roofing required to shelter the brand new cafeteria building. The crisis also threatened the supplies needed to fuel the heating systems in the Reptile and Tropical Houses.

In addition, Edward Heath's Conservative government was struggling to cope with the country's spiralling inflation. In an effort to curb it, a freeze in pay was announced, causing industrial unrest as wages were outstripped by the rises in living costs. Coal output was limited by the action of the powerful mining unions and commercial electricity consumption had to be rationed through the 'three-day week' at the beginning of 1974. The Wildlife Park fortunately suffered no power cuts, but had to take measures to reduce consumption, such as creating an eerie atmosphere in the Reptile House with low lighting. Indirect consequences, however, included the escalating cost of construction work. Inflation also forced entrance costs to be raised, at a time when families had less money to spend on leisure luxuries such as zoo visits. Country zoos such as the Wildlife Park, only accessible by car, took an additional hit with the rising cost of petrol. It is important to remember that the Park was not in a self-sufficient vacuum independent of the outside world. Like any business, as the venture grew, it also became more susceptible to problems affecting its consumers, with consequent fluctuations in visitor numbers.

At the end of 1974, therefore, a number of factors required the rapid expansion of the Park to be curtailed. At an important meeting called that year, the management's attention was drawn to the "serious financial position of the company". The overdraft stood at £70,000, a considerable level equivalent to some £540,000 in 2011, with more payments outstanding for ongoing building projects. With the Park under-capitalised, emergency action was taken to stop all development work for the next two years, with repairs restricted to a 'care and maintenance' basis.[60]

Mr Heyworth, moreover, was engaged in a draining struggle with local authorities over the general rates they demanded. He considered their assessed rates of the Park, since the transformation of the land use, to be unfair and extortionate. The sheer scale of the Park meant it would be impossible to find a tenant who could afford to pay a suitable rent, while its highly specialised layout prevented its sale for any other purpose. Drafting a letter in protest, he remarked he might be forced by rates and high taxation to close the Park and allow it to revert to the derelict state from which he had built it up, concluding that his words should not be looked upon as an "empty threat".[61] In a hostile economic environment, its future in a perilous state of uncertainty, Cotswold Wildlife Park was now to enter a period of frugality and consolidation, in stark contrast to the rapid growth of its first years.

Chapter 4

"Promoting a kindred spirit"

1975-80

By 1975, the land at Bradwell Grove had undergone a remarkable transformation. Cotswold Wildlife Park was a well-established Oxfordshire attraction, admitting a quarter of a million visitors each year. The basic existing layout was nearly complete, by will and necessity. More than 100 acres of the estate had been dedicated to the venture, but space was now limited and capital was not available for expansion. All profits were funnelled back into the care of the animals, through repair, maintenance and improvement of the exhibits. John Heyworth continually refused to withdraw any remuneration from the company. The attention of the staff was dedicated to refining what had been created and building a more widespread reputation. While major developments in the animal collection were frozen, therefore, these years witnessed considerable changes in the human aspect of the Park and its standing in the zoo community.

Brian Sinfield continued to oversee the everyday running of the Wildlife Park, in constant consultation with John Heyworth. The two men had fortunately formed a strong working relationship founded on mutual respect, although inevitably their ambitions for the Park meant that they got on one another's nerves occasionally. From the very beginning, Heyworth was keen to maintain possession over the venture but Sinfield particularly appreciated the independence that he was given in his role as curator. Through this freedom he gained a feeling of ownership in the project, a powerful incentive for any employee.[62] This drove passion and infectious enthusiasm in all his dealings with the Park. The staff had great respect for the energy of their immediate boss, affectionately nicknaming him 'Goonie', but also sometimes dreaded his appearance. Approaching in a flurry of ideas and activity, Brian would set them hard at work on a new project, which he oversaw for five minutes before leaving them to it as he attacked another job with vigour.[63] For the keepers, it was all a question of keeping out of his way to avoid being involved in his latest seemingly bizarre task – perhaps an unchanging reaction to management throughout human history.

For a man with a powerful artistic streak, Brian had been predominantly interested in the design and creation of the Wildlife Park. His personal enjoyment derived from the challenge of establishing its foundations and building it up, where his passions for wildlife, creativity and attractive display could all be fulfilled. After five years, and with a lengthy period of consolidation looming, he felt he had taken the project as far as he could. As John Heyworth had predicted upon his employment, a life of paperwork and administration held no appeal. He was such an integral part of the place, however, that his departure could not be immediate. From 1 November 1974, Brian's role was gradually reduced. He remained a director of the company and became a consultant on an annual retainer, spending a minimum of seven hours a week at the Park to offer advice and support. The arrangement was finally ended at the beginning of 1978, a little longer than was strictly necessary after the Park had arranged a new system of management. As John Heyworth explained in a warm letter to Brian, however, he had intended the consulting position as a means "to keep in close touch in the future... and also to show a small sign of the appreciation I have for all your help and friendship".[64]

Reflecting on his time at the Park, Brian described it as a very happy experience, especially as "doing something from scratch on that sort of scale was fascinating".[65] The job opportunity had been uncertain in 1969, requiring his new wife to give up her teaching job and move into a flat in the near-derelict Manor House with him. A great deal of time and energy then needed to be invested into the venture to make it a success. But at a relatively young age, the opportunity given by such a position of responsibility had been unique. He had also been able to travel extensively. As well as his trip to Kenya, he had been part of a zoo expedition to Indonesia in order to film the Komodo dragon. During a visit to the Seychelles, he had returned with a specimen of the largest and rarest nut in the world, the *coco de mer*, hoping Les Scott would be able to grow it in the Tropical House. Involvement in a zoo and its wider community was absorbing, dominating all his thoughts and actions, only infrequently interrupted by the political disputes and economic problems of the outside world. Ultimately, the original ambition he shared with John Heyworth had been achieved: to show animals in good, natural conditions and keep them well. Satisfied that the Park was in a self-supporting position, he embarked on a new challenge in the very different world of art dealership.

Between November 1974 and August 1975, Keith Cousins became a director and acted as general manager, helping Mr Heyworth oversee the running of the Park. Cousins had been offered a job as company secretary in December 1971, having become known to Heyworth through the prestigious Red Poll Cattle Society. He proved himself to be a competent administrator, controlling the gift shop, refreshment kiosks, wages, stores and public relations. Copies of acerbic letters written to companies or contractors, demanding explanations for delayed work or chasing up payments, suggest a ruthless efficiency. Managerial but characterful, he was nevertheless "not a zoo man"[66] and it became apparent he was unable to fill the large void left by the previous incumbent. Murmurings of discontent began to emerge among the animal keepers. It was not long before someone stepped forward to take centre stage, confident in his own suitability for the role.

A new curator

The new curator (see overleaf) was a leading light in the Association for the Study of Reptilia and Amphibia, an animal society based at the Park. This was founded in June 1977, aiming to promote "any necessary measures required to aid the conservation of all species of reptile and amphibian". This was to be achieved through fieldwork on British species and the promotion of captive breeding. The subtle

John Coborn: curator, 1975-81

John Coborn had arrived at the Park in November 1971 as the new reptile keeper. With the strict discipline he had gained while serving as an Army pest control officer, he stood in stark contrast to his predecessor Pete Walters, an entertaining but reckless Australian. Lacking in experience but very determined, he immediately got to work renovating the appearance and functionality of the vivaria. The Reptile House began to prosper, exhibiting a wider range of constrictors, pit vipers, crocodilians, lizards and amphibians. One of his enduring legacies was the installation of the grassed tortoise enclosure in the courtyard outside the Reptile House. Spare time beyond routine work for this project was limited, meaning it took nine months to construct. Completed in spring 1974, it housed the juvenile giant tortoises for several years, until they slowly outgrew it. Despite his obvious success in the Reptile House, however, John made no secret about his long-term career ambitions. He had expressed his interest in the curatorship to Mr Heyworth before the post was properly vacated by Brian Sinfield and, initially disappointed, had requested a reference for an equivalent position at Edinburgh Zoo in early 1975.[67]

His desire and persistence were rewarded when Heyworth asked him to become curator from 1 September 1975, in charge of all animal aspects of the Park. Further promotion to Director/Curator in 1979 granted additional responsibilities over the office and retail operations. A bluff and "burly animal lover with a military bearing",[68] *he brought a distinctive character to the position. The determination to establish order and routine formed a more defined role than had previously existed. Monthly typed reports to John Heyworth, for example, were among his first innovations. Park news, notable dates, animal births, deaths, arrivals and departures, staff changes and publicity events were all recorded in meticulous detail.*

He could sometimes rule with an iron fist, demanding ever greater responsibility and accountability from his staff. In his position, sternness was a valuable asset, especially when trying to manage the troubles and trials of a young and growing workforce, many of whom lived in close proximity to one another. Intensely loyal to the Wildlife Park, he could not tolerate lack of commitment or idleness. His brusque manner, nevertheless, masked a more social side of his personality. Will Manley remembered he had an unrivalled knowledge of curry houses and, after staff trips to other zoos, would be the first to suggest a spicy dinner and a drink. Keepers sharing his fascination for reptiles, such as Don Reid and Rod Lane, were more likely to witness a softer side to his temperament and a wicked sense of humour.

education of the public was also considered important. It was felt snakes and lizards had been subject to cruel myths for too long. They were to be liberated from their evil reputations and widespread phobias were to be cured. Each month, members from across the country would meet in the largest room above the Reptile House, the 'ASRA room', for slideshows, presentations and discussions. At this time, even zoo collections were relatively ignorant about the particular needs of their cold-blooded species. Breeding, especially, was the result of luck or basic trial and error. It was hoped that studies by the association would improve the situation, with communication vital for spreading their findings. Annual journals and monthly newsletters were thus published and John Coborn made prolific contributions to both, thriving in the committee-type atmosphere of the organisation. John Heyworth gave the society his full encouragement and support, not least with the provision of facilities at the Park, until dwindling interest forced it to close around 2005. In the early years, at the height of its popularity, ASRA greatly enhanced the reputation of its host. From this point on, the reptile collection was to become widely admired for its diversity and excellent standards of animal husbandry. By the early 1980s, the reptile keeper was constantly receiving requests for information and advice from collections and enthusiasts across the country, as his department was second only to the one found at London Zoo.[69]

Sharing expertise

By the late 1970s, there was an increasing drive among the zoo community to share expertise and collaborate to a greater extent. Zoo conferences were more common, allowing representatives from collections across the country to hear speakers present papers and discuss recent developments in the profession. On 1 May 1976, the first Cotswold Herpetological Symposium, on reptiles and amphibians, was organised and hosted by the Park. Proving to be a popular success, it became an annual event. By 1980, it had grown into the European Herpetological Symposium, so large it had to be moved to the Zoology Department of the University of Oxford. Several staff also attended the inaugural meeting of the Association of British Wild Animal Keepers, founded in 1974. They were encouraged to become members by John Coborn and became heavily involved, as much for the socialising as the aim of improving conservation through education.[70]

As yet, however, little consensus around an official organisation for zoo collections had emerged, so the Wildlife Park's involvement in these developments was relatively informal. It had withdrawn from the Federation of Zoological Gardens in Great Britain and Ireland in spring 1974, stating that "though the aims of the Federation were good, and that it has done a great deal over the last few years to help zoos, we felt that our policies were no longer in line".[71] Disagreements over regulations and courses of action had emerged, not least the Federation's opposition to any of its members allowing visitors to bring their dogs with them on their zoo visit. This restriction sat uneasily with John Heyworth, who was never without one or more obedient Labradors at his side. The Federation's annual membership fee, furthermore, was a fairly substantial expenditure at a time of necessary economies.

Mr Heyworth, nevertheless, had developed personal connections with fellow zoo directors, such as Molly Badham of Twycross, Victor Manton of Whipsnade and John Knowles of Marwell. They shared a similar ethos: the uncommercialised display of well-kept animals in near natural surroundings. Wildlife exchanges between these zoos became more common. The African waterbuck which arrived in 1976 were one such product of this collaboration, held in a paddock created between the lake walkthrough enclosure and the leopards. Mr Heyworth agreed to keep surplus males, which would be made available to other collections for breeding.

Barry Graves, a keeper at the time, remembered they could be particularly aggressive and troublesome. On one occasion, he was alone cleaning the paddock, sweeping the yard as he pushed his wheelbarrow up and down. The waterbuck was faced with this strange creature with two legs and one wheel, apparently challenging him for supremacy by its threatening parallel walk. Lowering its head, topped with two long, sharp horns, the waterbuck began to charge. In a vaulting display worthy of an Olympic champion, but with considerably less grace, Barry hurriedly managed to clear the high fence and escape with just a few bruises.[72] There was certainly no love lost when the species was eventually replaced, but the tale reinforces the human capability for amazing feats of athleticism when in danger.

Snakes on a plane

Despite improved British zoo collaboration, animal dealers remained the main method of acquiring stock. They would capture wildlife to order, or source them from collections abroad. Whenever John Heyworth went travelling, however, he would take every opportunity to supplement his own collection. He always enquired into the availability of native species and the feasibility of importing them. An interesting holiday to Thailand in March 1977 suggested this could produce varied results. He learned to his cost that not all foreign dealers were reputable: he lost a US$200 deposit, intended for a pair of white-handed gibbons.

More successful was the purchase of a number of exotic reptiles from a better known Thai contact, but a minor obstacle was encountered on the journey home. Keen to oversee the transportation of his new purchases personally, and avoid additional cost, John innocently sat on the aeroplane with a box resting on his lap, too large for the holdall. As they taxied towards the runway, a tired Australian air steward wandered down the aisle.

"Sir, may I ask what is in the box?" he enquired, suspicion aroused by the air holes. "Oh, nothing to worry about," came the casual reply, "only one or two snakes."

Gasps of horror rippled among the other passengers and the cargo was marched off the plane, with a loud but misleading protest echoing behind it: "They're quite harmless!" Once back in England, and never one to abandon a lost cause, he wrote a letter to British Airways, suggesting that they cover the shipping costs for the animals he was forced to leave behind. Although this approach unsurprisingly failed, the Thai authorities agreed to make all the necessary arrangements. When the reptiles finally arrived at the Park, the television coverage created by the saga provided excellent publicity.

The media attention was welcome, because national economic problems had continued to affect the Wildlife Park. In 1977, the government announced that inflation had pushed prices up by nearly 70% in only three years. Also that year, just 229,315 visitors passed through the Park's entrance gates, a record low figure, with dire consequences for profits and the capital available for improvements. The warning in 1974 from Keith Cousins had been heeded, and finances consolidated in that time, but further measures had to be investigated. An innovative promotion meant several complementary tickets were given to local schools, allowing free entry to a child but which obviously necessitated payment from their accompanying family. A number of special day events were also arranged to entice more people. A dog show had first been held in 1973, with categories including 'Most soulful eyes' and 'Waggiest tail'. Such pet shows were subsequently expanded and became popular attractions in the late 1970s. In addition, the grounds were made available to external organisations for the first time, particularly automobile clubs. The fields by the car park became host to hundreds of vintage cars and motorcycles as vehicle rallies gathered. Similar events have continued every year since.

More importantly, the possibility of partially converting the Cotswold Wildlife Park from a private company into a charitable trust was considered around this time. Rather than receiving any financial help from local authorities for his contribution to tourism, John Heyworth was still embroiled in a lengthy dispute with the council regarding general rates. An appeal in the Local Valuation Court was lost in May 1978 and an annual rate of £6400 upheld, causing him to write despairingly, "Are we to be crippled by taxation and very possibly forced to close?"[73] Forming a charitable trust was one solution with significant financial advantages, as demonstrated by his fellow zoo-founder John Knowles with the creation of the Marwell Preservation Trust in that same year. As a charity, Marwell was freed from the shackles of income tax, its general rates were halved and Winchester City Council provided a grant to cover the remainder. Such an arrangement, however, had considerable personal and emotional implications. A board of trustees was formed and John Knowles had to transfer everything – animals, housing, equipment, even the freehold of the estate land siting the zoo – to their control.[74] The previous owner became a single trustee among many and his influence in the running of the zoo was severely reduced.

John Heyworth was fully aware that following such a move would diminish his control of the venture, and the inheritance of his heirs. Particularly troubling would be the surrender of the ancestral home which the Park had been built to preserve. By the beginning of 1980, nevertheless, the consultant who had overseen the Marwell arrangement, Mr Barr, had been contacted and instructed to investigate the formation of a Cotswold Wildlife Trust. This would not transform the whole company, but instead create a dedicated section with an aim "to conserve and breed endangered species and to educate the general public in conservation and preservation". John Heyworth and John Coborn were to be honorary directors, along with Whipsnade's Victor Manton. The television naturalist David Attenborough politely declined an invitation to join the board, citing a lack of time and knowledge about the zoo business. The process had barely progressed beyond these preliminary stages, however, when they were advised that "the attitude taken by the Charity Commission [was] inconsistent with that taken in previous cases". It was not possible for entrance fees to be charged for exhibits.[75] As this was clearly a major stumbling block, the plan was shelved and the Park shouldered its tax burden to remain in the full control of the Heyworth family. At times, the draining of income to the Chancellor of the Exchequer was agonisingly frustrating and the pressure for charitable conversion remained great. The Heyworths, nevertheless, valued their independence and full influence over the Park's development too highly.

The Cotswold Wildlife Park Society

The Cotswold Wildlife Park Society, first conceived by John Coborn in 1979, was intended as a less complicated alternative to the formation of a charitable trust. The aim was to encourage a wide network of members to volunteer regularly at the Park, helping to fund the escalating cost of its upkeep. This was phrased in the official literature as "promot[ing] a kindred spirit among the Park's regular visitors". Their participation would allow them to become more informed and involved in future projects, while increasing the public's knowledge of zoology, botany and horticulture. For the adult membership fee of £7.50 a year, they would be entitled to free entry, a quarterly news journal, attendance at an annual zoological meeting, various other social events and the "opportunity" to help finance a conservation scheme. A short bulletin was published in the spring of 1979, including a profile on red pandas and news on Park births. The subsequent quarterly bulletins were more comprehensive, with written contributions from a wide array of keeping staff. A society committee was elected, rules and regulations drawn up and membership cards printed for issue. All that was required was a willing army of supporters.

Like some of the very best plans, the outcome was not the popular and money-saving success initially envisaged. Due to limited promotion, membership of the new society was disappointingly small. Among those visitors who did join, many held a different conception of their role, involving more benefits and less hard labour. There were plenty of volunteers for the evening socials but markedly fewer whenever a new enclosure had to be built or a new pool dug.[76] The membership card was sometimes seen by its holder as a pass granting privileged access to all areas. For example, a society member would simply wander into the penguin enclosure for a closer look, to the bewilderment and consternation of the keepers.[77]

In the Winter 1980-81 Society Bulletin, John Coborn praised the "slow and steady progress" made in two years and believed it had "the makings of a highly successful organisation in the future". This was his last editorial before moving on from the Park and, unfortunately, his successor as curator disagreed. Without Coborn's enthusiasm and support, the society met only a couple more times before quietly disappearing. Many of its constituent parts, such as animal adoption schemes and volunteer work, were revived later in the Park's history and became well-refined by the 21st century.

Pheasant breeding and the Insect House

As a result of the economic situation and limited resources, there were few major developments in the wildlife exhibits in this era, with two important exceptions. The first project worthy of note was situated in a space by the exit drive, opposite the Pets' Corner of the Walled Garden. There had been long-term intentions for its alteration and an opportunity presented itself when Keith Howman, secretary for overseas projects of the World Pheasant Association, contacted John Heyworth towards the end of 1978. He sought his help in a breeding scheme for the world's rarest pheasant species, whereby fertile eggs would be sent to their country of origin to be hatched and reared before being released into the wild. Nine aviaries were constructed at a cost of approximately £6000, with a quarter of this cost being covered by donations from some of the Park's regular material suppliers. The World Pheasant Association provided the birds and the information boards. Opened on 2 April 1979, species on show included the white-eared, blue-eared, Edwards', cheer and Mikado pheasants, with many breeding successes stemming from these humble beginnings.

The second project, the Insect House, initiated an even longer and more successful association. Since moving from Birmingham to the rural beauty of the Cotswolds at the age of ten, John Stone had developed a strong interest in all aspects of nature. He did not think, however, that he could form a career out of his greatest passion, butterflies. Several years were therefore spent as an engineer servicing vacuum cleaners, with every spare moment devoted to satisfying his enthusiasm for entomology. It was only in 1970 that he and a friend, John Midwinter, were able to establish the first butterfly house in the world, at Bourton-on-the-Water, Gloucestershire. It was through this enterprise that Stone met a school teacher called Michael Molesworth, who was also an acquaintance of John Heyworth. He encouraged Stone to make contact with the Wildlife Park, insisting that an insect exhibition created through his knowledge and expertise would be a very welcome addition. A meeting was arranged and Stone was shown a small, unpromising space available at the end of the garden centre, overlooking the car park. Fortunately, he decided to take up the challenge and became the first, and only, wildlife concessionaire at the Park.

It was agreed that establishing the new exhibit would be entirely Stone's responsibility and he spent the winter of 1975 building it with a friend, John Packer. Limited by the space available, the modest result opened the following Easter, with just a butterfly flight cage along a wall, several smaller exhibit tanks at one end and a shop space selling framed and boxed butterflies. It proved to be popular with the visitors, nevertheless, who were fascinated by the insects' intricate activities. Mr Heyworth was also pleased with the result, so much so that he agreed to give more favourable terms for Stone's contract. From that point, Stone received one penny for every adult visitor to the Park, as well as accommodation in an estate cottage to save the costly commute from near Cheltenham. This formed the foundation of a mutually beneficial business partnership which was to last until Stone's retirement nearly 30 years later in August 2005.

After a trial period of a couple of years, it was clear that there was considerable demand for a larger exhibition. John Heyworth took the decision to have a specially designed Insect House constructed. The chosen site was a space beside the children's playground, which then held a trio of Asian small-clawed otters. Stepping into the enclosure, he paced out the new area as the small mammals darted through the intruder's legs and nipped at his ankles. John Stone readily agreed to the suggestion that the Park would build the considerably larger exhibit space, while he would be responsible for the internal fittings. With characteristic urgency, Mr Heyworth had designs drawn up, more or less to Stone's specifications, and work began almost immediately. The front half of the Insect House was used as the shop where Stone derived a lot of his income, while the exhibits were installed at the rear. At that time, there was only one entrance and exit, so as much custom as possible could be attracted. A flight cage for butterflies, 50 feet in length, took up two complete walls, while an enormous leaf-cutting ant colony was housed in a central glass tank so people could walk all around it. The Insect House opened on 5 September 1977. Two nights later, intruders broke into the building, leading to the employment of the Park's first guard dog, a long-haired Alsatian called Heidi. Despite this rather inauspicious beginning, all expectations were soon surpassed and several exhibits drew a lot of attention. These included giant spiders, scorpions, stick insects and bees in a glass-sided hive.

Along with the breeding butterflies, the leaf-cutting ants were among the star attractions, and certainly one of John Stone's favourites. The nucleus of the colonies of two genera, *atta* and *acromyrmex*, had been brought from Trinidad by an entomologist friend. Two platforms were hung from the ceiling, with dishes of water surrounding the supports to prevent the ants escaping. A length of cord linked the leaves on one platform with their nest on the other, so visitors could watch the insects marching leaf cuttings across it. They had been installed in the flight cage of the original exhibit by the garden centre. One day, just before the transfer to the new Insect House, an overheating accident caused the fungus garden of the *atta* colony to dwindle and fail. As the new exhibit was being installed, the remains of the fungus were added to the *acromyrmex* colony. This act unintentionally caused it become a truly incredible size, larger than many found in the wild. Stone's skill ensured the colony thrived for many years but, when it eventually failed, a second colony was built from a nucleus used in the first filming of a queen ant for David Attenborough's *Life on Earth.* This lasted for 16 years, to Attenborough's later amazement, and the third colony was still going strong by the time of Stone's retirement.

By 1980, Cotswold Wildlife Park had encountered a few obstacles and suffered some setbacks, but had experienced considerably more successes. Like the ant colony, its working community had also grown spectacularly, with many keepers and their families living on the estate. After rapid expansion, the period of consolidation had guided the company on to more settled ground. While the Park society had disappointed with its limited number of volunteers, new animal exhibits had been efficiently introduced through prosperous and enduring partnerships. Most importantly, a reputation for attractiveness and high animal standards was becoming more widespread. There was a great deal of optimism, therefore, as John Heyworth and his staff entered the Park's second decade.

Chapter 5

"Improving on what we have got"

1980-1989

"There's a danger of spoiling it if it becomes too big, it is a question of improving on what we have got," commented John Heyworth on his Park's future in 1980. He was determined to maintain a balance between animal display, husbandry and natural surroundings, avoiding over-commercialism even as the Park became ever more popular. That year would welcome the 2,500,000th visitor since opening day, with more than 300,000 people now passing through the gates annually. The progress made had been extraordinary, beyond all original expectations, but the ambitious enthusiasm for perfection was unrelenting. Over the next ten years, standards across all zoos were forced to rise by increasing regulation and public awareness. The Park was generally at the forefront of this movement, offering well-kept animals, educational interaction and a number of new projects to interest a wide variety of people. Continual improvement was at the forefront of everybody's mind, from keepers through to the top levels of management.

The tenth anniversary celebrations began in January with the production of a limited edition first day cover. This was an envelope with a number of stamps issued for just one day, depicting several British wild birds. The main events, however, were held in fine weather on the last weekend of June, with the organisation of a

'Medieval Fayre'. The arrangements involved many groups from the Oxfordshire area, emphasising the Park's well-established links with local communities. School groups, for example, were invited to design and make a dragon to take part in a procession around the main display ring. Three finalists were selected during a preliminary round, with the winner chosen at the main weekend. The inter-pub tug of war was also received excitedly, particularly among regulars of nearby drinking establishments, who were always keen to engage in sporting rivalry. The winning team, from The Swan, Radcot, received a large barrel of beer, complimentary tickets and the 'prestigious' Cotswold Wildlife Park Tug of War Trophy. Over 5000 people attended the fair, where they revelled in traditional English entertainments, including knightly jousting, archery demonstrations by the Windrush Bowmen, Elizabethan buskers, dancing by the Bampton Morris Men, and a Punch and Judy show. Local craft stalls also offered goods and demonstrations, from spinning and pottery to bread-making. The list of possible celebrities to attend the event, and their fees, provides an interesting reflection on the popular culture of the time. According to a PR company, Jon Pertwee charged £600 (£2000 in today's money), despite finishing on the television series *Doctor Who* six years previously, while Peter Davison – soon to join *Doctor Who* but then known for *All Creatures Great and Small* – would set one back £450. Although Miss UK was available for £375, John Heyworth decided that it would be more appropriate for the zoologist and author Desmond Morris to present the prizes.

In 1981, after six years at the helm, John Coborn left the Park to take up a position as director of the Dudley and West Midlands Zoological Society. Although his disciplinarian manner sometimes caused tension with his younger and wilder members of staff, he had made many beneficial changes to the Park. He had remarkable self-confidence and a talent for personal promotion, enjoying regular appearances with snakes and lizards on television shows such as *Animal Magic* and *TISWAS*. His work, however, always reflected very well on his employers, contributing to the Park's widespread reputation, particularly of the reptile section. The Coborn family were a typical example of the community at the Park. Ingrid, his wife, ran the cleaning department with a similar efficiency to her husband, while their four children were involved whenever possible, helping

John Heyworth, founder of Cotswold Wildlife Park.
Painted by Andrew Festing, 1992

BRADWELL GROVE.

South and East Fronts.

FIRST EDITION.

By [illegible] of the Trustees of the late W. H. FOX, Esq.

=OXFORDSHIRE.=

Particulars and Conditions of Sale

A Most Attractive Residential, Sporting & Agricultural Estate

Well placed in the Heythrop Hunt on the borders of the Counties of GLOUCESTER and OXFORD. Four miles from Alvescot on the Fairford Branch of the G.W. Railway, about Eighteen miles from Oxford, and One and a half hours from London,

"Bradwell Grove"

Including a convenient sized MANSION in perfect order fitted with central heating, surrounded by broad Lawns, shaded by grand old Oaks and pleasantly situated in a

FINELY TIMBERED PARK.

A Recently Erected Steward's Residence,

EIGHTEEN FARMS

Some with Superior Farm Residences and Homesteads in good repair ;

Accommodation Holdings;

Modern Hunting Stables;

Together with the Advowson of the Parish of Holwell and Manorial Rights,

about **5,114** acres,

Renowned for its Partridge Driving,

WHICH WILL BE SOLD BY AUCTION BY

MESSRS. DRIVERS, JONAS & CO.

IN CONJUNCTION WITH

MESSRS. PAXTON & HOLIDAY,

At the CLARENDON HOTEL, Oxford,

On SATURDAY, the 17th day of SEPTEMBER, 1921,

At 2.30. p.m., unless previously Sold by Private Contract.

The Mansion and surrounding Farms containing 3,800 acres, forming a Renowned PARTRIDGE DRIVING ESTATE, will be Sold in One Lot, the remainder in several lots.

After the death of William Henry Fox in 1920, the estate of Bradwell Grove was put up for sale – these images are from the sales particulars. It was bought by Colonel Cecil Francis Heyworth-Savage

ESTATE OFFICE,
BRADWELL GROVE,
BURFORD, OXFORD.

TELEPHONE: BURFORD {2200. 3154

10th. April 1969.

B. Sinfield Esq..

Dear Sir,

Thank you for your letter and the references, which I am returning herewith. I have had a word with Mr. Bloom, who was most complimentary.

Very briefly, a few facts: This is a private estate of 3,500 acres, of which 1,500 are farmed by me with a farm manager, and of which 400 are woodlands. The remainder is tenant farmed.

We have a herd of Red Poll cattle, three brood mares, a flock of sheep, and approx. 950 acres under corn. We also have horses for riding. The wildlife park is to be in the grounds of the big house, which is empty, but in which there are to be two flats, one for the curator, and downstairs we intend to have a restaurant and gift shop.

I really want to go in for a wildlife park because I am keen on animals, but with farming becoming more and more difficult I hope to make it into an extremely paying proposition. Birds are to be the priority, building up a small stock of various animals by degrees, and the gardens will be important. I hope we shall be able to open to the public next Easter, and it is envisaged that we shall remain open from Easter to October.

I imagine that the best idea is for the curator to be paid a fixed wage, plus a portion of the gate money, and it would be necessary for him to be on duty throughout the summer, -- I'm afraid a considerable amount of secretarial work might be involved. John Taylor, from Cricket St. Thomas, is kindly advising me.

Apart from the week April 27th. to May 4th. I shall be here for the next two months, if you would be able to come and see us, -- provided you think our plans are of interest to you, and I should be very pleased indeed to meet you. Perhaps you could suggest a date?

A 1969 letter from John Heyworth, summarising his vision for the new wildlife park, after he had invited Brian Sinfield to be its first curator

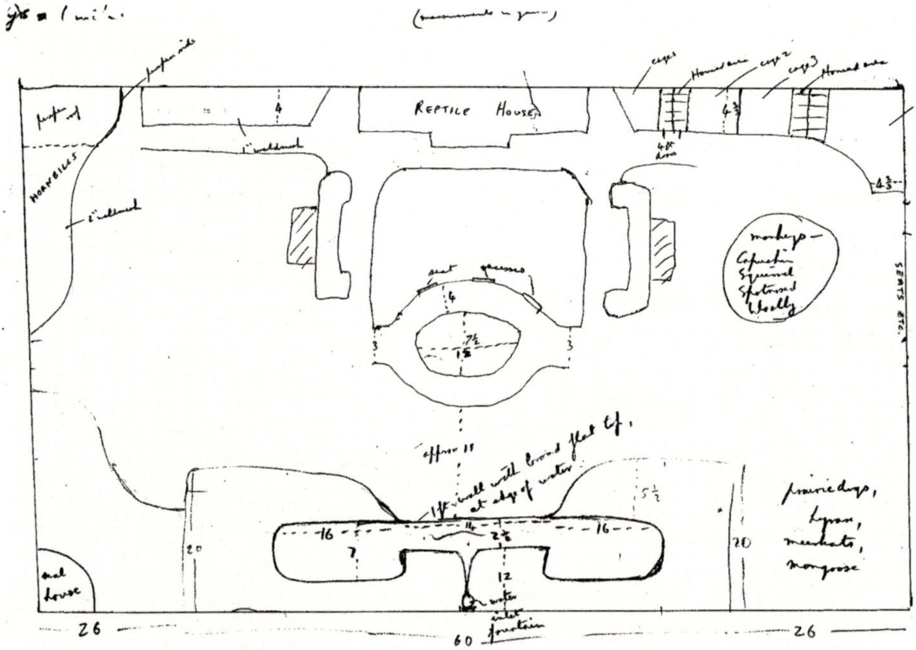

Above: John Heyworth's original sketched plan for the layout of the Walled Garden.
Below: a map from the 1971 planning application to create what became the African Plains.

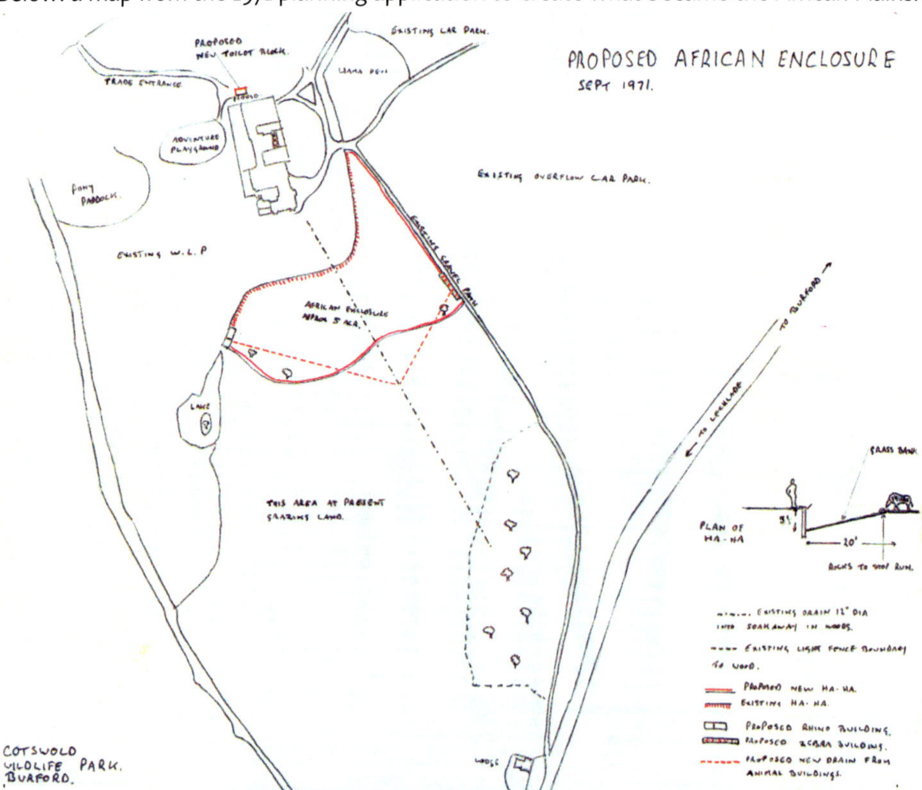

COTSWOLD WILD LIFE PARK IS TO OPEN AT EASTER

WITH THE constant arrival of birds, animals and reptiles to the Cotswold Life Park, near Burford, and the workmen busily preparing the grounds and buildings, all is proceeding well for the Good Friday opening of this very welcome addition to the amenities of West Oxfordshire.

This new venture is being set up by Mr. John Heyworth on part of his estate at Bradwell Grove. It is not a zoo because the animals will be able to roam in large enclosures and the free-flying birds will have large open air aviaries.

The finishing touches are being put to ponds and pits, and shrub planting, turf laying and path laying are in hand. Mr. Heyworth and the Curator, Mr. Brian Sinfield, are confident everything will be ready for the first visitors at Easter.

Some 60 acres of the park will initially be open to visitors although it is hoped eventually to utilise the full 3,500 acres of the estate.

Already many animals and birds have been housed in their quarters while others are being held in readiness to be moved in as their abodes are completed.

One corner that is sure to be popular with the children is the pool shared by the baby seal and the penguins. Another popular feature will be the glass-sided tank for otters which is in a very attractive setting that includes a waterfall.

Eagles

Other animals will include Indian porcupine, raccoons, red pandas, a wallaby, a llama, North African sheep, a rhea and monkeys.

Among the numerous species of birds are flamingos, toucans, giant hornbills with wing spans of over five feet, herons, eagles and peacocks.

In the reptile house and crocodilium will be lizards, crocodiles, alligators, terrapins, tortoises, and snakes. There will also be an open air area surrounded by a moat and a wall for other snakes.

Pony rides

It is hoped to breed from the animals and birds and thereby build up the numbers gradually.

Apart from the areas containing wild life there will be a picnic area, ornamental gardens, and an adventure playground for children set among trees. At weekends children will be able to have rides on donkeys and ponies.

Ample car parking space is available and there will be a restaurant in the Manor House as well as a gift shop which Mr. Sinfield's wife, Mrs. Ann Sinfield will look after.

Educational

There will also be a lake area for water fowl, ducks, geese and swans and a pets corner where children will be able to wander among animals such as rabbits.

Mr. Sinfield will have four keepers in charge of the animals and there will be a permanent staff of gardeners.

It is also intended to make natural history educational facilities available with lecture rooms and films available for students.

Mr. Sinfield has had a wide experience in zoos, both at home and abroad, having been at Chessington Zoo and the Ministry of Research Flamingo Park. He also spent five years at the Taronga Park in Sydney, Australia.

Mr. Sinfield has been at Bradwell Grove for seven months preparing the wild life park.

Natural settings

He has worked with animals since his school days and has specialised in large mammals.

The aspect of animal work he enjoys most is setting up zoos and the like and at Bradwell Grove his flair for designing the animal pits, pools, aviaries and other areas is clearly seen in the attractive and natural settings he has constructed.

Many people from all parts of the country are expected to visit the park for what should be an ideal day out for the family.

Workmen putting the fnishing touches to one of the huge aviaries in the walled

Early publicity for the Park in 1969 and 1970 and (inset above) the Park's first poster, showing its entrance fees of 5 shillings for adults and 2 shillings for children

WITNEY and West Oxfordshire GAZETTE

THURSDAY, MAY 22, 1969

WILD LIFE PARK OPENING NEAR BURFORD

Free-roaming animal and bird life

Story by ARTHUR LARNER

A WILD life park is to be established near Burford.

It will be on part of the Bradwell Grove Estate, which is the home of Mr. John Heyworth and his wife, and is due to be opened at Easter time next year.

Its inhabitants will include animals which will be able to roam virtually free in large enclosures, free-flying birds in large open-air aviaries, reptiles and fish. As the build-up develops according to the support received, so will depend what future animals and birds will be on show.

Work in hand

Outline planning permission for the project has already been received, and preliminary work is in hand. Mr. Heyworth whose idea it was to open part of his estate for this purpose, emphasises that it is not a zoo he will be opening, as everything will live in spacious natural surroundings.

He feels it will be opening up the countryside for the townspeople and yet retaining its natural beauty.

The project should certainly be a great attraction for visitors, as it is in the middle of a tourist centre. The estate adjoins the north-south Banbury-Swindon road, and it about three miles off the main A40 Oxford-Cheltenham road from Burford, which is known as "The Gateway to the Cotswolds."

An outline of the plans was given today by Mr. Heyworth and his estate manager, Mr.

Above: brand new aviaries in the Walled Garden. Below: the popular Pets' Corner "reached saturation point in a very short time with so many people confined within its walls" and was extended for the Park's second season in 1971.

The Park's first two curators, Brian Sinfield (above) and John Coborn (below)

The Walled Garden has always been a focal point of the Park. The original garden was choked with brambles when plans for the Park began in 1969. Pictured right from top: Ann Sinfield, wife of the first curator, in the newly cleared garden; the new garden under construction; the Walled Garden in the early 1970s; an aerial view from the 1980s. Left and main picture: the flourishing garden today

Above, reptile keeper Don Reid in the original tortoise enclosure in the 1980s. The Park's keepers enjoy educating visitors while on the job. Right, Doug and Dennis Wilks work on building the leopard enclosure in 1981 – whatever the weather

Maintaining the Manor House is an important part of the Park's work – the top picture shows repairs to the roof in 1988. It has also been a family home for John and Susan Heyworth, above, and their children. Left: the Manor House interior

Reggie Heyworth, who took the reins as managing director of the Park from 1995

A Children's Farmyard had replaced the original Pets' Corner in 1984, but in turn this needed improvement. An important project in 1992 was the construction of a new farmyard barn, which included an incubation room where visitors could watch chicks, ducklings and goslings hatching. The pictures show how the site was transformed

The walkthrough Madagascar enclosure, created in 2007, transformed an empty area between the Walled Garden and the car park

After the death of two of the Park's original white rhinos, and the third well into old age, younger animals were acquired in 2009

The pictures show Ruby and Nancy (who were sourced in South Africa) arriving by lorry and exploring their new home

John Heyworth had long held an ambition to include giraffes at the Park. In 2010, this was finally realised in time for the Park's 40th anniversary. Three males, Koife, Century and Wallace, arrived to enjoy a spacious house (with an elevated walkway for visitors) and a large paddock

The middle two images show the giraffes arriving for the first time

with litter picking, car parking and guidebook selling. It was not an easy decision for John to leave his position as Curator but the difficult challenge of restoring Dudley Zoo's fortunes proved too appealing. His new position, unfortunately, did not prove as happy or enduring. Coborn's later correspondence with Heyworth describes a string of unsatisfactory jobs, including caterer, publican, market stall holder and night security guard.[78] By 1986, however, he had emigrated to Australia and forged a successful career as an animal writer and editor, utilising the experiences he gained as author of many articles for Park publications and ASRA newsletters.

The arrival of tigers

The first major animal project of the new decade brought one of the largest big cats, the Bengal tiger, to the Park. John Heyworth had considered the introduction of such an exhibit for a number of years. Towards the end of 1978, he wrote to the oil company ESSO, which famously used the animal's image as an advertising logo, to suggest they sponsor an enclosure at the Park. Their rejection, however, meant that the Park had to wait a while longer, until enough of its own funds were available. This fortunately coincided with Molly Badham's offer of two cubs born at Twycross in 1980. In March, work began on an enclosure behind the leopards and beside the Bactrian camel paddock. The male, Sultan, and the female, Begum, were first shown to the public when John Heyworth's youngest daughter, Joanna, opened the new Tiger House on 17 November 1980. Rod, their keeper, recollected that the male had a devious streak, with unpleasant consequences for any unwary visitors. Prowling up and down the cage until a large crowd had gathered, he would then turn and spray them with urine. The nostril-burning smell ensured friends and family of any unfortunate victims kept away for days.[79]

The new exhibit, unfortunately, can be seen as a misstep in the Park's development. The rectangular cage had a solid wooden frame, barbed wire overhang and two separate sections in the adjoining house. It certainly did not match the natural surroundings of the rest of the Park. Many visitors were unsettled by the pacing of the tigers, which they perceived as an act of frustration and boredom. They preferred the nearby leopards, in an enclosure that had been renovated and improved in 1981. The amount of space given to the

Robert Golding: curator, 1981-83

Robert, or Bob, Golding became the new curator in March 1981, the only time a candidate was hired from outside the existing keeping staff. Bob's early interest in animals had been nurtured through frequent trips to Bristol Zoo and a growing friendship with a reptile keeper there. He had earned a considerable amount of experience while building up a zoological garden at the University of Ibadan in Nigeria, from 1963 to 1979, before returning to the UK as curator at Chessington Zoo for two years. He had a more direct approach and modern outlook than Coborn. This was required to adapt to the regulations changing zoos at that time. There was also a need to bring the Park into the wider European and global zoo community. Bob particularly encouraged members of staff to attend the growing number of symposia, to learn from the papers presented. He then insisted that the participants returned to the Park prepared to give a lecture on the content to their colleagues. These experiences built confidence in public speaking and emphasised the increasing importance of interacting and engaging with visitors, at a time when keepers' skills in public relations were a neglected area.[80]

It is often difficult when outside management is dropped into a close, working community. Bob appears to have elicited mixed responses from the staff at the Park. One keeper remembered getting off on the wrong foot, initially too busy to help move Golding's furniture into his new flat, then trampling mud into the pale carpet when he finally volunteered.[81] *Moreover, the relationship between the curator and the head gardener, always notoriously difficult due to different priorities and interests, was heightened at this time, particularly regarding the renovation of the Tropical House.*[82] *Other colleagues, however, remember good relations with a characterful man. They praised his effective work in getting everything ship-shape, particularly financially, with the overdraft paid off and debt avoided. His talented wife, Peaches, was also widely admired for her work overseeing the Park's publicity. Their time at the Park was relatively short, however, and they moved away in November 1983.*

tigers was also disliked, with the general feeling that it was too small. As was frequently explained in response to complaints, tigers travelled long distances in the wild because they had to hunt for food, but this need was removed in captivity; in fact, their enclosure was among the largest in the country. When the male and female were separated after fighting, furthermore, the concerned public suggested they needed company, unaware that they were typically solitary animals.

From this experience, John Heyworth and his staff became increasingly aware that balancing animal husbandry with public perceptions, however misinformed, was a crucial challenge in maintaining a reputable zoo. On one level, this was a welcome shift from the demand for pure entertainment that was associated with visits to zoo menageries in earlier years. Ground-breaking natural history documentaries such as *Wildlife on One*, first broadcast in 1977, and Attenborough's *Life on Earth*, which followed in 1979, helped educate the wider population and ensured their greater discernment about zoo standards. On the other hand, it could also fuel unrealistic or incorrect expectations for animal husbandry, sometimes leading to hostility against zoos. Considerable effort was still required to spread the message of the Park's valuable work.

Expanding the Tropical House

The transformation of the Tropical House, begun in 1981, was far more successful. Expansion was necessary after the exotic plants had outgrown the building renovated ten years earlier. Completely dismantling the original structure, a larger glass house was built on the same site, 25m long and 9m wide. A high, arching roof offered more internal volume for botanical life than had been allowed by the previous sloping top. While the new building was being erected, head gardener Les Scott fervently hoped that the well-developed tropical plants could be preserved following their exposure to the cruel outdoor elements, and his prayers were answered. The *bougainvillea* and *plumbago* once again proved how hardy they were along with many other flowering plants such as *hibiscus*, angel's trumpet, *thunbergia* and *abutilon.* A number of interesting crop plants, such as sugar cane and banana, were added to these. Before the Tropical House was opened to the public in 1982, many birds were introduced to fly among the tree tops. The original species of hummingbirds, sugarbirds and white eyes returned, along with new additions such as the grey-breasted sabrewing and tanagers.

In a large pool beneath the branches of the Tropical House, the Park's pair of Mississippi alligators, Albert and Fiona, lurked. They had previously been kept in the Reptile House, where they occasionally mated but failed to hatch a clutch of eggs. It was hoped that the greater environmental controls available in the Tropical House would lead to successful breeding, although this did not prove to be the case.

The alligators were the favourites of their keeper, Don Reid, who could summon them at will.[83] He had been instrumental in the planning and design of their new accommodation, including a passage through to a grassed outdoor enclosure for use on sunny days. Chains over the doorway allowed the alligators to go out into the open air but prevented birds from flying out. An inspection by the Federation of Zoological Gardens in 1983 commended this "noteworthy exhibit of crocodilians". One final touch involved the erection of a sign in the pool: "Please do not throw coins at the alligators." Human nature, encouraged by a few carefully placed pennies, ensured this became an effective way of earning tips.[84]

Under the guidance of Don, the Reptile House itself continued to thrive and grow. He had arrived in October 1976, having previously run a fishing tackle shop in Coventry while keeping reptiles in a shed in his back garden. He had heard about the position through the International Herpetological Society and was encouraged to apply by the Park's reputation. Don initially had to manage the whole department on his own, sometimes a lonely job as the layout of the Park meant that he was separate from the other animal sections. By 1978, however, the growing number of specimens required the hiring of an assistant to share the workload. Over the years, the position was filled by committed enthusiasts such as Les Edmonds, Beverly Brett and Glyn Evans. Working from the solid foundation created by John Coborn, Don was influential in advancing the keeping knowledge of reptile husbandry and breeding, although he stressed that this was largely a matter of trial and error. Without widely accessible scientific information, it was continually necessary to study, read and experiment. Communicating successes and failures with other zoos and private owners was also vital. The result of this dedication was a well-respected collection, notable for its diversity of reptiles, ranging from geckos and iguanas to the Gaboon viper, rainbow boa and the Aldabra giant tortoise.

The exhibit spaces were a crucial contributing factor to this professional standing and indeed one of Don's favourite aspects of his job was reworking the displays in the winter, which he tried to change fairly often to keep them looking fresh. Having trained as a technical illustrator, he had a certain artistic awareness and this provided an outlet for his creativity. As many of his cold-blooded charges were more dormant in this season, he was able to invest a lot of time and effort into the aesthetics, which were greatly appreciated by the Park's visitors.

For the herpetological world, the early 1980s was an exciting period of discovery and enlightenment, in which Don felt privileged to be involved through his work at the Wildlife Park. He had briefly left the position in March 1979, to take part in a friend's new locksmith business, but immediately regretted the decision. Fortunately his replacement was not a success and he had returned in August, securing a better house on the estate in the process. By March 1986, however, he was feeling restless and came to the conclusion it was time to move on. His success in breeding tortoises at the Park created an opportunity to travel to Madagascar, where he worked with one of the most endangered tortoises in the world, the Angenoka, for the next ten years.

The departure of Bob Golding marked the beginning of a long new era for Cotswold Wildlife Park, as Colin Fountain was promoted to the helm. He began his new duties on 14 November 1983 and remembered the greatest change being the mountains of paperwork he had to face. There was always a danger of getting 'bogged down' in bureaucracy. Colin, nevertheless, ensured that he always followed his true interests and got out into the Park to know the animals, in order to spot any problems. He was determined to be a hands-on curator, remaining involved with the animal keeping, and always close to the troops on the ground. His philosophy was never to ask an employee to do something he would not do himself. If he felt distant from any area or section, such as the Reptile House, he would endeavour to become involved and fill any gaps in his knowledge.[85] This style would inevitably cause friction and occasional clashes of personality, but the Park could only benefit from Colin's tenacity and dedication.

Challenges for the zoo community

As much as attractions such as the Wildlife Park were increasing in popularity at this time, so too were the numbers of their detractors.[86] The 'Zoo Check' campaign was launched in 1984 by the film stars Virginia McKenna and Bill Travers, who had found fame in the 1966 film *Born Free*, about the life of the naturalist Joy Adamson. Their aim was to "fundamentally change the way we treat

Colin Fountain: curator, 1983-2002

A small man with distinctive facial hair, Colin was always driven by an uncontainable zeal for his job. Having begun his working life in the carpentry trade, a local animal keeping opportunity arose when the Duke of Bedford opened Woburn Safari Park in 1970. Here Colin gained his first experience caring for wildlife through a role in the children's zoo, complete with supposedly appropriate animals such as lion cubs, bear cubs and cobras. It was here too that he met his partner, Maria. She had started work caring for the dogs left in the kennels at the safari park, before working up to a keeper role. Visiting Cotswold Wildlife Park one weekend in the early 1970s, they "just fell in love with it" and returned as often as they could.[87] In 1975, Colin enquired about available keeping positions and, a week after an initial rejection, he was invited to interview for a new vacancy.

Colin began work as a keeper, looking after the small mammals and birds in the Walled Garden, or bottom section. He made his first step on the promotional ladder, however, after only a few short months. Ken Lock, the head keeper of top section, left for a job in Suffolk and Colin gratefully accepted the vacant position. His new responsibilities included the animals in the African Plains paddock and the walk-through lake enclosure, allowing him to form strong relationships with several of the larger characters. The strongest emotional bond was formed with the exceptionally tame white rhinos. The original pair, Somtuli ('Bull') and Lebombo ('Bella'), had been joined by another female, Ukhukho ('Paddy'), in November 1977. They were so gentle that Colin was able to climb on to the big male and ride on his back, illustrating both the rhino's calm nature and the lack of health and safety concerns at the time.[88]

Care always had to be exercised, however, and the same animal was the source of one of his luckiest escapes. A keeper's life is always precarious and a lapse of concentration could prove fatal. On this occasion in 1979, Colin was alone doing a late shift, shutting the rhinos away for the evening. Entering the yard with the trio, he herded the two females into their pen in the house as normal. As one of them was in season, Bull was being uncooperative and wished to follow, while his keeper wanted to take him to his own pen. Stepping over the large horn to find some extra space, Colin suddenly found himself catapulted 15 feet into the air and then slamming back down into the ground. Quickly managing to scramble over the concrete wall, he escaped with severe bruising and a stiff body for weeks.[89]

In the autumn of 1983, Colin was enjoying a day off when John Heyworth called at his cottage and offered him the position of curator. He was the obvious candidate, as the most senior keeper and having built up an extensive knowledge of the Park's organisation when working closely with Bob Golding.

captive wildlife", making it their mission to investigate zoo conditions and campaign for improvements. The ultimate goal was to phase out the existing concept of the zoo completely, with a shift in focus to conservation of natural habitat and the preservation of indigenous wildlife.

While there was much to be praised in their aspirations, their idealistic approach prevented collaboration with animal attractions. Zoo Check failed to differentiate properly between poor quality zoos and their better counterparts, which promoted good husbandry standards, education and conservation efforts. This created conflict with the Federation of Zoological Gardens. "It is a great pity," commented the editorial of the Federation's 1985 newsletter, "that an obviously talented group of people cannot direct their efforts to something more constructive in support of the wildlife and conservation world."[90]

In order to counter this sort of hostility, the zoo community underwent a number of transformations. First, the Federation absorbed its rival group, the National Zoological Association, to become the sole society representing British zoo interests. It stressed its two main aims were the proper care of wild animals in captivity and increasing support for conservation by breeding, education and research. The organisation also believed that there should be some legal control regulating animal collections, therefore lobbied for the Zoo Licensing Act, passed in 1981. As the government refused to fund an independent inspectorate, zoo professionals carried out the inspections now required every three years. While obviously not a perfect solution, it was better than nothing and helped eradicate the truly abominable attractions that still lingered.[91] Requiring a demonstration of its commitment to animal welfare and high standards, Cotswold Wildlife Park rejoined the Federation in September 1983. It also became a member of the marketing committee, to help present the aims and successes of zoos to the public more effectively.

Along with the tide of increasing regulation of this nature, John Heyworth continued to maintain a strong interest in the running and public perception of his Park, determined to ensure high standards were preserved. He always attended the monthly section heads meeting which Colin Fountain had established upon becoming curator. In these gatherings, the leaders of every department, including gardens, retail and hygiene, could report news and raise concerns. As well as being regularly informed by official occasions such as these, Mr Heyworth was a frequent sight striding around the Park, with his impeccably trained Labrador gundogs in tow. Unanimously described as the "perfect country gentleman", he would take these opportunities to talk to his staff, in an endearingly self-effacing and slightly restrained manner.

He would take interest in any task they were doing, sometimes volunteering his services. On one occasion, a group of keepers was working with some branches in an aviary when he came along and offered to help. Pulling back some wire to allow more room, a branch sprang back and trapped his fingers. "Excuse me," he said after a short silence in which the keepers dared not smile, "I've been rather silly... Can someone help get my hand out?"[92] While his background meant he was never a 'man of the people', and social distance was always maintained, he cared sincerely about the Park and everyone in its community.

While he felt exhibit standards were high, moreover, Mr Heyworth constantly sought ideas for new attractions which would suit the surroundings. These were needed in order to enhance the collection and keep the visitor experience fresh. In 1985, he agreed to help with a coursework exercise by a group of third year estate management students from the Royal Agricultural College. Working from a concise brief, the students were asked to write an individual report on the Wildlife Park and the surrounding land. In their work, they offered some suggestions for improvements to attract new visitors. For example, links should be developed with the education departments of Gloucestershire, Berkshire and Wiltshire county councils, to encourage school groups from a wider area. The advertising budget should be increased to £30,000, with more emphasis on leaflets and posters in local hotels to attract seasonal tourists. More special day events, car rallies and fairs were also recommended.

Many of these ideas were subsequently implemented, although a few of the more ambitious schemes were disregarded. An audio-visual 'rainforest experience' walkthrough building was disregarded, for example, as dangerously close to a capital-intensive, theme park-styled attraction.[93] Heyworth continued to be guided by his long-standing principle that the Wildlife Park should remain an affordable, relaxing and enjoyable experience for all, with animals and good animal husbandry at its core.

The Children's Farmyard and Bat House

The Children's Farmyard, created in the winter of 1984, was the next major project for the Wildlife Park. All the animals from the original Pets' Corner were transferred to a patch of land between the lake walkthrough enclosure and the adventure playground. The vacated area made available in the eastern end of the Walled Garden was then landscaped by Les Scott. This included a koi carp pond, with pens also constructed for common marmosets, cotton-top tamarins and red-bellied tamarins. Aside from the welcome additional space, the new farmyard was not a drastic alteration from its predecessor. Children were still allowed to mix freely with the domesticated animals. Geese, ducks and bantams wandered the yard, while pigs, lambs and Humphrey the tame llama were all behind simple fenced barriers. Various breeds of rabbit and guinea pig, diverse in appearance, were placed in open top hutches to prevent harm from too many small, grasping hands. Nearby, children could enjoy a ride around the paddock on a pony or donkey, an existing popular attraction run by Ken Bedford, a well-known local character from Burford. The farmyard was opened at Easter 1985 with a fancy dress competition, with prizes for the best costumes awarded by Pam Ayres, the famous local poet. Although lacking the more unusual species that had inhabited the Pets' Corner in the 1970s, such as porcupines and woodchucks, children were fascinated by the tame animals and the area quickly became a firm favourite of visiting school groups.

The following year, another new attraction was built to accommodate some less cuddly creatures. The old cart barn that stood opposite the Reptile House had been used as a maintenance workshop since before the Park's opening day. In the early years, this domain was ruled by an 'old-school' and very skilled carpenter called Ted Greenaway. Everything from enclosure frames to carrying boxes was built and repaired here, always following the make-do-and-mend spirit.[94] By 1985, however, John Heyworth wanted to complete the reptile courtyard with animal exhibits and began considering possible ideas for this remaining building. Eventually it was decided to convert the barn into a bat house, with two floors offering different perspectives into the glass-fronted flight cage. An eerie darkened atmosphere was created, with tree branches for roosts installed against a forest mural backdrop painted by a local artist, Mark Amis. The intention was to create a hybrid environment to accommodate two species, the rainforest-inhabiting Indian fruit bat and the smaller Egyptian fruit bat, which preferred to settle in open caves and old buildings. The choice seemed to work particularly well for the breeding record of the latter. Ten years after Rod Hull and Emu, old friends of the Park, had opened the Bat House on 17 May 1986, a group of 40 Egyptian fruit bats had grown to over 300 individuals.

Encouraged by countless interpretations of *Dracula*, bats have long been associated in the public mind with bloodsucking and defenceless women in nightgowns. Despite the Wildlife Park's best efforts to educate, some misunderstandings endured: keeper Maria Fountain remembers entering the enclosure one morning to start cleaning it out, only to find a large Indian fruit bat had fallen from its roost and was stranded on the floor. Stepping beside it, she allowed it to start clambering up her body, using the hooked fingers on its wings, so it could climb back into the tree. As Maria stepped into the light, with a bat's wing outstretched over her face and its head close to her neck, she did not know early visitors had started entering the Park. Two women stared in horror at the spectacle unfolding through the glass, before taking deep breaths and beginning to scream hysterically in unison about a vampire attack.[95] Escapades such as these have entertained keepers during their tea breaks across the years.

Less success was enjoyed by a holographic exhibition, trumpeted as the latest technical innovation, which was installed in a neighbouring room. This closed after a year due to a disappointing financial return. Then in 1989, Colin Fountain invited Philip Williams, an exceptionally talented glass-blower, to set up a workshop in this space, where he has now been for 23 years, delighting visitors with his craftsmanship.

The longest and most expensive building schemes ever undertaken at the Park involved no animals at all. The restoration of the Manor House roof between 1986 and 1989 was one of many projects that would not attract publicity or visitors but was simply desperately necessary. English Heritage had made the Bradwell Grove Manor a Grade II listed building in 1985, meaning it was of special historic interest and warranted efforts to preserve. This distinction ensured John Heyworth received his first ever financial public grant in relation to the Wildlife Park, after many unsuccessful requests for various proposals. The £2000 received from West Oxfordshire District Council, however, was a drop in the ocean compared to the overall cost of the essential work. A chartered surveyor was required to oversee the lengthy project, as local building contractors Wilks Brothers repaired the roof, remedied structural weaknesses and restored the crenellations. After three years' hard labour by Doug and Dennis Wilks and their team, in a relatively smooth process only occasionally punctuated by problems, there was no longer any danger of leakages, falling masonry or total collapse. John Heyworth's lucky streak continued, moreover, with a £10,000 grant from the regional tourist board being allocated for various upgrades to the facilities in 1987. An extension to the cafe, a rain shelter with picnic tables by the tiger enclosure, improvements to the adventure playground, further car parking and a new toilet block near the playground were added, with obvious practical benefits to visitors.

Record attendance

These additions were vital to cope with demand because, by the late 1980s, the Park was reaching the peak of its popularity. Writing in the editorial for the 1988 newsletter, Colin Fountain commented on his pride at the steady growth of visitors "at a time when most zoological gardens are justifiably concerned at a drop or levelling off in attendances". Over the next three years, the annual attendance record was repeatedly broken, until an unbeaten 376,412 people visited in 1990. Throughout term-time, the main car park had to be reserved entirely for coaches, in order to cope with the vast number of school parties flooding through the gates. Cars were instead diverted to the grass verge.[96] In the gift shop, a wealth of pocket money was willingly passed over the counter to purchase cheap, colourful plastic toys. The innumerable crowds of kids, all grasping, jostling and shouting, were succinctly described as "daunting" by the overwhelmed ladies struggling at the tills.[97] During the holidays, the school groups were replaced by hordes of tourists. Now the workers in the pay hut became the front line, desperately trying to keep the endless stream of cars flowing. John Heyworth would sometimes visit here on busy days, to give a helping hand and also marvel at the cascade of cash keeping the company's finances healthy.[98] With the nearest competitors such as Woburn, Longleat and Twycross being over 70 miles away, the Wildlife Park had a solid catchment area for local visitors. Crucially, however, word about the attraction had spread far and wide, enticing people from across the country.

Always helping to fuel this interest were promotional features in local and national publications. In April 1990, Michael Stourton, a journalist and family friend, provided an article for the *Financial Times*, offering a neat summary of the Wildlife Park's achievements on its 20th anniversary. If John Heyworth "seems almost too laid-back to be the central figure of such a vital and successful enterprise," he wrote, "this impression is entirely false". He had actively pursued his interest and animals were only included if he thought they would prosper in the surroundings. "A personal touch and inspiration" was always apparent, enhancing the appeal of the whole place.[99] Over the past 20 years, the Park had grown considerably in staff, space and specimens yet retained its personable and friendly character. Dedicated keepers and management had improved standards for an increasingly interested and discerning public, while participating in a more collaborative and organised zoo community. In a letter to Mr Heyworth, Stourton had also complimented the Park's "relaxed atmosphere of informality" and "complete absence of the institutional".[100] This had been a constant throughout the Park's existence and was clearly something valued by the visitors, as they returned in their droves. The challenge for the next decade was to retain this feeling while developing the professionalism of staff and company, necessitated by the pressures of a changing world.

Chapter 6

Accidents and achievements

1990-1999

The new decade did not start well for John Heyworth who was sometimes rather accident-prone. On several occasions when meeting staff in the Park, he would walk backwards away from a conversation, continuing to talk, and would stumble on some unseen hazard. He would then pause and continue as if nothing had happened. This could not be the case at the beginning of 1990, when a more serious incident occurred while he was out pigeon shooting.

Climbing over an obstacle but forgetting to empty his gun, he slipped and the weapon inadvertently fired, shooting him through the foot. Struggling back to his green Subaru, bleeding profusely, he managed to drive back from the old airfield on the other side of the A361 using one foot. Unable to negotiate any obstacles very carefully, the quickest and most direct route home involved smashing through a closed gate. With blood pouring from the wound, Susan Heyworth patched him up in their kitchen as best she could before taking him off for more help. Later that afternoon their son Reggie returned to a deserted house, his father's gun on the kitchen table, blood all over the floor and trailing from the wrecked Subaru, to find a message in his mother's handwriting: "Darling, Dad has shot himself in the foot. Gone to Burford Hospital. Please could you clean his gun!" Upon John's arriving at hospital, the sympathy of an animal-loving nurse quickly evaporated when she heard the full story.[101] After a few weeks confined to a hospital bed, he returned home. Despite the severity of the accident, he was soon patrolling the Wildlife Park again, albeit on a quad bike with his foot resting in the air.[102] The tale quickly entered folklore as a perfect illustration of his indomitable character.

Although the owner was out of action, a more hierarchical system of management had built up over the years that allowed the Park to function fairly smoothly in his absence. By that time, Colin had become known as the general manager, which was a more unambiguous title to the outsider than 'curator'. He was responsible for the everyday running of the Park, including retail operations, and was well able to keep in control of every situation. Simon Blackwell worked beneath him as assistant curator, helping to oversee the animal department, a position he held from November 1988 until his departure in 1998.[103] The division of the animal keeping staff continued, with separate animal kitchens and tea rooms depending on where people worked in the Park. At this time, there was a section head, deputy head and assistant deputy for each area. Terry Hornsey oversaw the top section, with Mike Woolham and Rod Lane as his respective subordinates, while Ron Hurley ran the Walled Garden, assisted by Dave Edgington and Mike Downman. Since Don Reid's departure, Nigel Platt had managed the Reptile House, where he had been joined by Glyn Evans in June 1986. Although there was good social mixing and friendly rivalry, there was rarely any need to get involved in the workings of another section, unless one was a relief keeper.

Illness strikes the penguins

Disaster of a different kind struck at the end of 1990, when a mysterious illness affected the penguins. Since the first ten Humboldt penguins had arrived from Peru in 1970, their pool in the Walled Garden had become perhaps the most popular attraction at the Park. They were joined by four rockhopper penguins in 1972, distinguished by their yellow tufted 'eyebrows'. Visitors found the antics of the small, comical-looking birds entertaining and large crowds gathered for penguin feeding time at 11am and 4pm each day. Initially there were few signs of breeding but from 1979, Martyn Williams, a likeable and long-serving keeper, had developed a very successful hand-rearing technique for the Humboldt penguins. Left to their own devices, the chicks of captive birds would rarely live to a fortnight, often succumbing to a respiratory fungus disease called *aspergillosis.* By removing the eggs, personally caring for the chicks and introducing the adolescents to the group, Martyn ensured that the majority survived. His practice was developed and refined at the Park in the 1980s, communicated to other zoos and became the subject of a very successful symposium. A penguin-rearing house was built next to the pool and opened in 1986, where work in the incubation room was on public display. With a breeding group of more than 20 birds and a regular surplus being supplied to other collections, this year proved to be a peak.

There were signs of trouble from 1987, with lighter hatch weights, higher chick mortality and lower fertility. By 1990, keepers were distraught to find the group's condition worsening and their numbers diminished rapidly. By December, just one weak juvenile remained alive; Percy was the Park's only penguin for six months, and had to be carefully hand-reared, forming a strong mutual attachment with the keepers. The tragic backstory made Percy famous in the local media, ensuring he received letters, cards and even tins of sardines from well-wishers. It was not until much later that it was discovered 'he' was actually a female. The first investigations into the cause of death of his fellow penguins proved inconclusive, but eventually suspicion fell on a number of pollutants isolated in all the birds during post-mortem. Polychlorinated biphenyls (PCBs) and dieldrin pesticide, possibly originating from their diet, could accumulate over the years, causing infertility and acting as an immunosuppressant. In order to remove any possible problems in the future, the entire enclosure was stripped and renovated, with additional barriers to prevent children feeding dangerous material to the birds.

The penguins may never have returned to Cotswold Wildlife Park, as speculative plans were afoot in July 1991 to accommodate a group of Baikal seals in the remodelled pool. However, they proved expensive and difficult to acquire, and five Humboldts arrived instead from Penscynor Wildlife Park, Wales. Unfortunately, health problems and deaths continued over the next few years, to the bafflement and frustration of their keepers. Much money was spent on enclosure improvements but, in late 1994, a breakthrough was finally made with the isolation of Avian malaria in one bird. A course of anti-malarial drugs was prescribed and the colony slowly recovered, with a group of nine arriving on breeding loan from other British zoos in the summer of 1995. The following year, their forces were strengthened by the arrival of a pair of king penguins. After a tumultuous period, their breeding prospects once more looked promising.

The 1990s recession

National economic problems, meanwhile, were causing considerable concern for the Park, as the country entered recession in the early 1990s. Inflation and rising interest rates had a major effect on consumer confidence, while levels of unemployment grew steadily worse. Trips to zoos and wildlife parks were once again a luxury that many could no longer afford. This proved to be a very difficult period for everyone involved in the zoo community. Cotswold Wildlife Park proved to be no exception. After record visitor numbers, Park attendance plummeted by over 60,000 in two years as school trips in particular declined dramatically, with a knock-on effect in the summer holidays compounded by families tightening their belts. At the end of 1992, Colin circulated a memo, warning that "due to the financial position of the Park in the present recession, cutbacks are inevitable".[104] The implication for staff was that all overtime ceased with immediate effect until further notice. They were, however, more fortunate than colleagues at Kilverstone Hall in Norfolk, where Lord and Lady Fisher had kept a small wildlife park, with a particular emphasis on South American species, but rising costs and falling visitor numbers forced it to close in 1991. With great regret, they had to distribute their animals to other collections. Fortunately the Park managed to weather the economic storm with little long-term damage but the experience of the Fishers provided a severe warning.

Despite the unpromising economic environment, the Park's policy remained "a programme of continual improvement".[105] The Insect House, built in 1977, was first on the list for a number of alterations when funds were available. John Stone felt the butterfly flight cage did not work well, as it was not wide enough and just a few species acted completely naturally in the small space. He maintained an impressive breeding record, nevertheless, and it was only when the roof began leaking in 1990 that real change was required. Renovation work was continued throughout the winter, with least disruption to the public, but the fiercely cold temperatures caused the deaths of many of the invertebrates. The most important exhibit, the leaf-cutting ant colony, was preserved with a polythene sheet covering and an electric fan at both ends blowing hot air into it, before they were moved from their central tank to a special side display. Stone's troubles, however, did not end with the completion of the construction work. He had requested a simple double-glazed top for the flight cage but the architect had designed a plasterboard ceiling with just two windows installed. The butterflies, therefore, were attracted to these points of light and would not fly, breed or eat. This created a long and arduous challenge to remedy the problem. Stone had also suggested the reduction of his shop area, to allow for larger exhibit space, but public sentiment now turned against the boxed butterflies he sold to supplement his commission income. He had successfully defended the practice in the past, arguing that the necessary breeding in butterfly farms helped wild species, through the release of surplus stock and the preservation of rainforest habitats. This time too many public concerns were raised and, after renegotiating his contract, he instead began to sell artificial spiders, toys and other more accepted products.[106]

After struggling to overcome the problems with the butterfly flight cage, Stone eventually decided to introduce another species into the space. Obtaining four golden orb web spiders from an Essex breeder, he hoped they would construct their large and complex webs from silk which shimmered gold in the light. In the wild, these can be so big and strong that they entangle small birds. Several large circles of thick vine were installed, to act as a foundation for the webs, and the first spider was introduced to its new home. It quickly started work and, in just two hours, built a sticky fly trap 75cm across. Although Stone added the other specimens, carefully watching for any signs of cannibalism, only the original spider seemed able to spin webs. Whenever she completed one, she was pushed off it by a larger rival, until all were finally accommodated. The impressive display eventually included over 100 females and a pint of maggots had to be added weekly, to provide enough fruit flies to feed the spiders. Unfortunately the mess created by this diet caused the exhibit to be unsustainable, with the plants dying and the display gradually deteriorating in appearance.[107] Nevertheless, visitors young and old continued to enjoy the other unusual 'creepy crawlies' on show.

The Reptile House was another area looking tired and in need of a facelift after several years in its existing layout. The first job at the end of 1990 was to extend the crocodile exhibit to the rear of the main building, constructing on top of their rarely used outdoor enclosure. In late 1992, the other exhibit spaces were also stripped and renovated to provide more convenient and varied vivaria. A South American rainforest atmosphere was created in one area, with tropical plants and misters to help with humidity. Dwarf caimans, lizards and tortoises from that continent were put on display. By 1985, the giant tortoises had moved to their current pen adjacent to the African Plains paddock, so the outdoor courtyard was made available for smaller breeds. The aquarium building was increasingly part of the reptile section's domain, accommodating larger snakes such as the reticulated python and anaconda, as well as aquatic reptiles such as the Malayan box turtle and Caspian terrapin. The tropical marine collection was less impressive, with only a number of colourful but typical fish on display, although the guidebook saw fit to mention a particularly fine specimen of the African lungfish. In autumn 1993, Nigel Platt moved away from the Park to take up a new position and his long-serving assistant, Glyn Evans, was promoted to replace him. Under his guidance, more venomous reptiles were included in the collection, such as Gila monsters and red spitting cobras, requiring much greater attention to safety than some reckless habits of the Park's early years.

In 1992, alterations to the Children's Farmyard were the major priority, despite the slump in visitor numbers. The area had been very successful since it had replaced Pets' Corner but it was felt more could be done to utilise space. A large barn was constructed, with a high sloping roof and many open-top pens on either side of a central aisle. By the entrance, the public were able to watch eggs hatching through the viewing windows of the incubation room, and then see the progress made by the growing chicks, ducklings and goslings. A collection of old farming tools, many salvaged from the farms of Bradwell Grove estate, decorated the walls and ceiling. Outside, the paddocks had been extended to cover three acres and more animal breeds were added, including Shetland ponies, Angora goats and pygmy goats. The dwarf zebus, miniature versions of the sacred

Indian cattle with a distinctive hump on the shoulders, were an unusual sight alongside the Vietnamese pot-bellied and Oxford sandy and black pigs. A letter was written to Princess Diana, inviting her and the two young princes, William and Harry, to a tour of the Park and the opening of the new barn, but they declined. Unfazed by the lack of a royal visitor, and the accompanying publicity, the revamped attraction was opened in March 1993 to hordes of delighted children.

The Park newspaper

The same year, a group of keepers demonstrated their independent initiative by compiling a newspaper for the Park. Over several months, Mike Downman encouraged and cajoled some of his colleagues to contribute articles on subjects that they were particularly interested in. The idea was to offer a more intimate look behind the scenes, something that would clearly be enjoyed by regulars and could also entice new visitors to return. They had been inspired by an original Park magazine, *Wild Life Park News* , first published in September 1970 and sold for just one shilling. Twenty-three years later, the first edition of *Talk on the Wild Side* was available for 25p. Features included a profile of John Heyworth, a report on the Park's barn owl reintroduction scheme and information on tiny poison-arrow frogs. A centre-fold section for children, called 'Chatterpiller', was a departure from the original, containing a crossword, competitions and animal facts. The edition proved to be a success and became an annual publication, enjoyed by contributors and readers alike. The current design has barely changed since it was rebranded as *Wild Talk* in 1996, although colour photographs were introduced from 2000. Finally the public could see their favourite animals, and keepers, in their full glory.

The Park commemorated its 25th birthday with a special edition Silver Jubilee newspaper, with many articles and pictures reflecting on its history and looking forward to the future. The actual celebration was held on the weekend of 10 and 11 June 1995, with a more global, multicultural theme than the Medieval Fayre of the Park's tenth anniversary. To build interest and excitement, special bonus tickets were placed randomly in the dispenser, offering admission at the equivalent of 1970 prices: 25p for adults and 10p for children. Among many craft demonstrations, the Adams Axemen displayed their forestry and lumberjack skills, plus a falconry display was performed by Geoff Dalton, a long-standing associate of the Park. Magic shows, storytelling, a carousel and the Humble Pie Puppet Show Theatre entertained the children. The Park reverberated with the contrasting sounds of the Chedworth Brass Band and the Peruvian Chan Chan music of the Andes. A conservation marquee included a table full of items to be touched and handled, including illegal elephant tusks confiscated by Her Majesty's Customs. Even during a celebration, the Park sought to raise awareness about poaching and the habitat destruction threatening animals in the wild. Informing and educating in memorable ways had become a major part of the Park's purpose, mostly inextricable from entertainment.

As Colin Fountain pointed out in the commemorative newspaper, the Park had changed progressively but the general layout and some of its original residents still survived. The female great Indian hornbill and Harry the male tapir had their regular admirers. It was two spider monkeys, Lady and Gertie, who could claim the most affection. Native to Central and South America, the Park's group could be found in a large enclosure on the path between the Manor House and the Walled Garden. With no opposable thumbs but a prehensile tail acting as a fifth limb, they would frequently perform acrobatic acts to the delight of visitors. Maria Fountain developed a deep emotional bond with these animals and would hand-rear their abandoned youngsters, which required an extraordinary amount of time and effort. As the babies needed constant bodily contact for at least a year, Maria was well known for going about her day with a hairy monkey clinging to her. They were even taken to the local supermarket, hidden under a bulky jumper, until the visits had to stop when attempts at banana pilfering began.[108] She was acutely aware that it was essential to raise them as an animal, and not treat it as a child or pet, but the final separation was always heart-breaking.

Maria, arguably, had a rival for the person most dedicated to the spider monkeys. Daphne Rogers was a pensioner and Park regular, who could spend hours sitting and watching her favourite animal, ignoring everything else on display. She particularly loved Gertie, with her distinctive chocolate brown fur and piercing blue eyes.

Although Daphne lived miles away in Herefordshire, with no easy means of transport and a very small income, she was determined to visit frequently. Setting off at six in the morning, she would have to take three different buses to arrive at the Park for lunchtime. On one occasion, she started chatting about her visit to see her "adopted daughter" with a neighbouring passenger. Reaching into her purse for a picture, she beamed with delight when the person overcame the shock of seeing a hairy monkey and politely declared, through fixed smile, how beautiful she was. Upon her arrival, Daphne would seek out the monkeys' keeper, initially Maria then Bryan Taylor, to ask how they had been getting on. She would then hand over the tin of pineapple that she always brought as a present for Gertie.[109] Such devotions may be at the more extreme end of the scale, but this lady's story provides the perfect illustration of the affection and long-term loyalty that Cotswold Wildlife Park could inspire in thousands of its season ticket holders and regular visitors.

Ageing animals

By the mid-1990s, however, the circle of life unfortunately meant that many of the Park's earliest animal characters began to succumb to old age. Mary, the Brazilian tapir, had reached an impressive 28 years before she died in autumn 1993. During that time, she had borne 12 calves, ensuring countless generations lived on in other British and European zoos. Fiona, the Mississippi alligator, also passed away, as a result of egg peritonitis, an internal complication with the abdomen which was difficult to treat. Another female from a Suffolk collection was introduced to Albert, but after a long amicable relationship with Fiona, he did not take kindly to the stranger and attacked her viciously. The decision was taken to move Albert on to the Welsh Mountain Zoo where, in new unclaimed territory, he was less aggressive. One advantage of the alligator departure was that ground birds such as Luzon bleeding-heart pigeons, ringed teal and African jacanas could be added to the Tropical House without fear of them becoming a tasty snack. The new resident reptiles, the rhinoceros iguanas, proved to be no threat and largely ignored the bustle of birds and visitors.

On the other side of the Park, the future of the elderly tigers, Sultan and Begum, was also uncertain. As early as May 1992, minutes of a meeting show the section heads were considering what animal exhibit should replace them, although they were granted a reprieve two months later. Despite the adequacy of the enclosure, public perceptions were often hostile and concerns about its available space were mounting. As much as Colin Fountain tried to defend it, he had to admit the rectangular pen with its prison-like fences was "not necessarily in keeping with the rest of the Park".[110] When funds finally became available in the middle of 1994, an improvement project was given the green light and planning began in earnest. Colin and his staff went on research trips to several other British collections to investigate big cat enclosures built in the previous decade. The intention was to learn how these facilities worked for both the animals and the keeping staff, thus drawing from the best examples and avoiding costly mistakes. Construction work began in spring 1995, with the complete demolition of the old enclosure. The new one was to be approximately four times the size of the original and, rather than imposing wire fences, large glass viewing areas were installed. This barrier was safer, more aesthetically pleasing and gave the public closer access to the majestic animals, although the windows meant more cleaning work for the keepers. During winter and wet weather, the tigers could shelter in a smaller, more practical, house with a separate pen intended as a cubbing area.

Lions replace the tigers

After all the investment and painstaking care taken over the project, the tigers were unfortunately unable to enjoy their new accommodation. During the building work, they had taken a 'holiday' to the holding quarters of Longleat Safari Park. Construction of their housing was made a priority, so that they could return as soon as possible. At the end of November, they were brought back to be kept indoors while their outdoor enclosure was completed. Shortly after, their keeper Rod Lane started his shift one morning to discover Sultan had died peacefully in his sleep at the good age of 16.[111] As it was too dangerous to introduce a new mate to the naturally solitary tigress, she began her 'honourable retirement' in the cubbing area while the Heyworths pondered their next step. They eventually decided to introduce one of the world's rarest big cats, the Asiatic lion, to the Park. Two young males arrived in March 1996, one later being exchanged for a female to make an unrelated pair. The aim was to join five other British collections by participating in the international captive breeding programme for the species. Sabu, the male, threw himself into this arduous task with enthusiasm, fathering many cubs over the coming years. The rest of his time was apparently dedicated to trying to hunt his keeper down. While this might be disconcerting for most people, Rod chuckled fondly as he remembered the animal that "spent most of the day trying to work out how to kill me".[112]

Elsewhere in the top section, the walkthrough enclosure also required urgent attention. Years of accumulated leaves and sludge meant the lake needed dredging in the winter of 1994. Most of the water had to be gradually pumped out then an infestation of red-eared terrapins removed. These had been donated to the Park a decade earlier by a breeder and had multiplied beyond expectations, but their voracious appetites had an unwelcome impact on the chicks of the resident birds. Once given the all clear, a mechanical digger rolled its way into the mud and began slowly shovelling the detritus into a small dumper truck, which removed it from the site. After many long weeks of this messy task, the lake bottom was then re-lined with blue clay and gradually refilled with rainfall. Although costing well over £11,000, the flamingos and waterfowl could now enjoy much clearer and safer water. Further into the woodland, about 15 wallabies shared the central paddock with the rheas, flightless birds from South America. Across the path, the capybaras remained separate from the Park's new pair of Brazilian tapirs, Timmy and Squidge. The tapirs had quickly become as beloved as their predecessors and were also making a good start on matching their breeding success. By the turn of the century, however, the area and its displayed animals were largely unchanged from 30 years earlier.

While there were few major new exhibits appearing across the Park in the later 1990s, two articles from the *Wild Talk* newsletter show that efforts were channelled into enhancing animal husbandry. In 1996, the spotlight was placed on the ten aviaries by the scimitar-horned oryx enclosure near the exit drive. The original partnership with the World Pheasant Association continued to be successful but these birds were also joined by colourful touracos and hornbills. Over the previous year, keepers had been busy re-landscaping each aviary to echo the natural habitat of its residents. For example, a terraced rockwork with three steep levels was constructed for the Himalayan monals and snowcocks, which liked to climb, perch and nest up high. A Scottish pine forest was also introduced to encourage the breeding of the rare capercaillies, inhabitants at the Park since autumn 1992. This included an adjacent aviary connected by a tunnel too small for the male, in which the female could escape his boisterous attention if necessary. Keepers at the Park were always learning on the job and were eager to put those lessons into practice. Their involvement in regular enclosure renovations, particularly aviaries, ensured constantly improved conditions for the animal.

In 1997, another newsletter feature explored the work used to supplement the experience of captive animals, in order to prevent laziness and encourage physical activity. Environmental enrichment, as this was increasingly being called, had been practiced in zoos before an official term existed for it. However, efforts had been increased and more innovative schemes introduced since the 1980s. The intelligent tamarins, squirrel monkeys and lemurs, resident in the east end of the Walled Garden, particularly needed fulfilling challenges to keep them engaged. Food was scattered in hidden places around the enclosure, encouraging the creatures to forage among the grass and tree bark. Three small feeds a day, dispersed in this manner, also forced more activity and exercise. Occasionally, coconut shells packed with rice, potato and mashed banana were included as a tricky puzzle with a tasty reward. The keepers constantly experimented with new methods, such as nutty treats held in unstable, mesh-lined hanging baskets. Although all these animals had been born in captivity, a responsible zoo was dedicated to offering as natural a life as possible. Attention had always been paid to providing appropriate environments and "enrichment" for its animals, but the accumulated knowledge was helping increase husbandry standards and breeding successes.

For much of the decade, therefore, life at the Park continued routinely along a plateau, overcoming periodic crises as they were encountered. Visitor numbers stabilised following the recession, staff were comfortable and animal exhibits rarely altered. Under Colin Fountain's dedicated management, construction work was focused on repairs and upgrades to existing displays and the all-important, if unseen, infrastructure. It was felt that the general layout was appealing to visitors and there was reluctance to make any additions that might disturb the functioning status quo. When change was forced by an ageing exhibit, the result was generally simple replacement or renovation, rather than complete transformation. A new generation of leadership, however, was emerging on the horizon, brimming with energy and adventurous ideas. Like Colin, they wished to protect the fundamental principles at the heart of their workplace, but they were also driven by a desire to regain some momentum in its development. This approaching new era featured a profusion of large, exciting projects, in a burst of activity second only to the initial foundation of the Park.

Chapter 7

"Don't do what is new: do what is never old"

2000-10

Since John Heyworth reduced his involvement from 1995, the running of the Park was placed in the safe hands of Colin Fountain, the general manager. He was diligent in his duty, making sure he knew the detail of every event or issue. As a result, the Park continued to be well-maintained and respected. The momentum, excitement and innovation of earlier years, nevertheless, diminished slightly. It took new characters, with different ideas, to build on the solid foundation and try to realise its potential. They helped lead the Park into the 21st century and consolidated its place as an exemplary modern zoo.

There were some early but isolated exhibit changes under Colin at the beginning of the decade, prompted mainly by necessity. The De Brazza monkeys had first arrived at the Park in 1977 and were located in an enclosure behind the Reptile House courtyard. With the death of the old female in 2000, the lone male was retired to Howletts Wild Animal Park in Kent and the keepers began to consider possible replacements. It was decided that a pair of siamangs, the largest member of the gibbon family, would be the newest additions. These black-furred apes are native to the lowland forests of Indonesia and have large throat sacs, which they inflate to produce loud, resonating calls. Their outdoor enclosure, surrounded by old sycamore and yew trees, was enlarged and furnished with exciting climbing equipment. More radical, however, was the closure of the Park's aquarium to provide extensive indoor quarters for the siamangs. After 30 years, the aquarium was looking tired and neglected in comparison to other areas of the Park, so the small collection of tropical fish was donated to other zoos. The renovated space allowed visitors to observe the resident apes closely through the glass windows. Over the next ten years, the siamang group bred so successfully that many of the animals in the co-ordinated captive breeding programme (EEP) were subsequently related to the Park's pair.[113]

At the beginning of 2001, all planning at the Park was interrupted by the grave threat posed by a national crisis, the outbreak of foot and mouth disease. This highly-infectious, viral disease affects cloven-hooved animals, causing high fever and blisters on the feet and mouth. Spreading rapidly across the British countryside, over 10 million sheep and cattle were slaughtered in an attempt to stop the infection. On 27 February, eight days after the first case was detected, Cotswold Wildlife Park was closed to the public and remained shut for more than five weeks. The virus could be transported by visitors and several species at the Park were susceptible to it. Although zoo animals did not need to be automatically slaughtered, an outbreak on site could have been devastating. Even when it was safe to re-open, the Park had to buy expensive disinfectant mats for visitors to drive and walk over. The whole situation had a harmful impact on the year's visitor numbers, which dropped below 300,000 for the first time since 1978. The reduced revenue meant a small financial loss was incurred in 2001.

Reggie Heyworth

By this time Reggie, son of John Heyworth, was more involved in directing the Park. When the Park opened in 1970, he had begun working there at the age of eight, selling guidebooks to earn pocket money. According to his mother, he had a very persuasive sales technique, trapping drivers by leaning against car doors as they parked then asking innocently if they would like to purchase a brochure.[114] He studied history at Lincoln College, Oxford, before working at an investment bank in London and Hong Kong between 1983 and 1990. He then took the life-changing decision to take a job in Tanzania as a tour guide, escorting tourists on safari. This eventually led to the opportunity to participate in a Tanzanian government conservation programme with the Frankfurt Zoological Society, studying the critically endangered black rhinoceros. Three and a half years were spent working with the programme, including a year living among the rich wildlife of the Ngorongoro Crater. Upon his return to thc UK in 1995, familial duty and his passion for animals encouraged Reggie to immerse himself once again in the Cotswold Wildlife Park, as managing director.

Reggie had never run a business before and found the whole experience to be a steep learning curve, especially after spending such a long time out of the country. He therefore describes the development of the Park between 1995 and 2000 as "relatively uneventful".[115] He concentrated on addressing the significant overdraft, improving the Park's infrastructure and staff accommodation, and returning the Park to a sound business foundation. Moreover, he fundamentally agreed with his father's vision and had great respect for Colin Fountain's work in maintaining it, so did not want to make any radical changes. The experiences of other zoos and the leisure industry in this period provided a stark warning. Vast sums of money were being invested in entertainment attractions following the hype and popular fashions of that time. In 1994, Cricket St Thomas in Somerset, an early inspiration for Cotswold Wildlife Park, had themed itself around Mr Blobby, the bumbling pink character from the popular but ephemeral BBC show *Noel's House Party.* This was forced to close after just a few years as fans lost interest. Reggie's oversight of the Park has since followed a simple mantra: "Don't do what is new: do what is never old."

By the turn of the century, however, Reggie was more experienced and he had learned a lot about the zoo industry. He inevitably grew in confidence and ambition, forming his own views about the Park and how it could be progressed. Tim Miles, the new head gardener appointed in 1998, shared that energy. He had been selected by the Heyworths to raise the profile of the gardens, building on the work of Les Scott, his predecessor, who retired after 30 years in 1999.[116] Tim seized the opportunity to introduce exotic planting to this corner of the Cotswolds, co-ordinating it with the surrounding animals. His enthusiasm for horticulture, however, was not necessarily shared by the more conservative animal keeping staff, and he faced some resistance among colleagues in realising his ideas. The most challenging part of the job in his early years, therefore, was convincing others of the value of horticulture for improving the Park as a whole.

After 27 years of dedicated service, Colin Fountain left the Park at the end of August 2002. Since becoming curator in 1983, he had led with authority, dedication and constancy. His promotion to general manager had meant he oversaw all departments, from animals to retail and maintenance. This was a role he took very seriously and he made every effort to learn as much as possible about each area. Over the years, however, the Park's staff had grown more numerous and diverse. The needs and pressures of the disparate sections within the company necessitated a different working culture. Reggie was personally keen to take full responsibility as managing director at the top of the hierarchy, with individual department managers focusing on their particular area of expertise. Colin and his wife Maria moved to Somerset, where they continued to work with animals at the Secret World Wildlife Rescue centre.

The position of general manager was therefore retired and Dave Edgington became curator from September 2002, supervising all animal-related matters. He loved the Wildlife Park, and recognised the immense value of its existing form, but also felt that the place

Dave Edgington: curator, 2002-08

Dave had first arrived at the Park as a keeper in December 1983, after working at nearby Birdland, Bourton-on-the-Water, for four years. He was the obvious choice for the curator's position with experience of the Park at every level, having risen through the ranks to assistant curator. In addition to a passion for his work, Dave also pursued a number of interests in his spare time. He moonlighted as a guitarist in the Park band, 'Jinxed', which often played at social functions to the delight, or dismay, of their colleagues. Dave was also a keen amateur historian and was the first to research the Park's past. In 2005, he wrote a short history of the animal collection, which provided a valuable stimulus for this book. As curator, however, he had to grapple the most with the Park's future. Shortly after taking the job, he described how his initial amazement at the offer was "almost immediately replaced by excitement and terror in equal parts".[117]

had remained static for too long. He knew that changes and a large amount of work were required to realise its full potential.

Some of these developments had already begun in the Walled Garden, during Dave's time as head of this section. He built a successful partnership with Tim Miles and the two planned a number of important changes in this area. With their enthusiasm and innovation, they were able to persuade Reggie of the benefits of the alterations. The first project involved the conversion of the area in front of the Tropical House. A small island to be inhabited by a pair of blue and gold macaws was created, surrounded by a moat and climbing plants. Next, an expansion of the meerkat enclosure in 2001 allowed a more appropriate desert theme to be developed, through the use of spiny cacti and artificial rockwork.[118] From these experiences, the new curator was confident in his ability to take all the animal exhibits forward in closer co-ordination with the gardens department. Other keepers and staff were encouraged to think more innovatively, contribute ideas and be creative about proposals. The shift in culture provided considerable momentum for change and the opportunities created by good design, horticultural skill, caring animal husbandry and imaginative planning seemed to be limitless.[119]

Improving reptile and tropical displays

Under the leadership of Reggie and Dave, therefore, a number of improvements and new exhibits were designed and realised. Firstly, Marc Ormond, who had arrived as head of the herpetology department in April 2000, undertook to transform the entrance of the Reptile House. He hoped to create diverse and interesting exhibits by displaying several species in a single enclosure. In early 2003, he chose to install two 'aqua-vivaria', which had bottoms like tropical freshwater aquariums but with heated land areas on top. The tanks were made entirely from glass and took three weeks to build to the Park's unique design. Two heavy-duty stands, made from thick steel, also had to be constructed and bolted to the floor. In one tank, several tropical fish, such as South American tetras and discus, lived alongside a vegetarian fly river turtle. Several chameleons and some unusual tree frogs lurked in the plants above. In the other aqua-vivarium, freshwater stingrays and an arrowana swam below another species of chameleon and some day geckos. The whole foyer was then repainted and decorated with vines and leaves to create the environment of a lush tropical rainforest. Elsewhere in the house, the crocodile enclosure was refurbished to prepare for the arrival of a pair of Morelet's crocodiles in December 2003 and four years later the Park's investment was rewarded with the first ever UK breeding of these rare reptiles.

In 2004, the re-glazing of the Tropical House gave the opportunity to redesign the interior. Although many bird species flourished in the existing environment, they were elusive and many visitors were disappointed as they walked through the enclosure. By April, all the flora and fauna had been stripped, so the keepers sought to rebuild in a way that would improve both the visitor experience and the well-being of the resident birds. The area was beautifully landscaped with waterfalls leading into a large shallow pool, a perfect habitat for small waders. Moss-covered tree stumps were strategically placed so that birds would perch in full view. Speckled mousebirds, Mount Omei babblers and Luzon bleeding-heart pigeons were returned, along with many new additions such as ground-dwelling Scheepmaker's crowned pigeons and wading jacanas.

The garden staff performed some miraculous work once again, transforming the space from work site to tropical jungle in just three months. Epiphytic ferns, bromeliads and insectivorous pitcher plants were grown along a network of twisted oak branches salvaged from the estate's woodland, while a variety of shrubs and climbing plants offered cover and nesting opportunities for the birds. In 2006, a pair of Linne's two-toed sloths arrived to clamber slowly through the overgrowth, well-camouflaged by their mossy fur. Despite the extensive work, old plant favourites survived, with the established bird of paradise flower (*strelitzia reginea*) protected and the elephants' ears (*alocasia esculenta*) replanted. The newly installed sprinkler system created a tropical mist every 15 minutes, benefiting planting, birds and the general ambience. The improved enclosure aided the husbandry of the resident creatures but also immersed every visitor into a vibrant sensory experience of sight, sound and smell.[120]

A number of bird species were, moreover, the central feature of a new area next to Bradwell Grove miniature train station, opened at Easter 2005. Despite the husbandry and breeding successes of the aviaries in the original pheasant area by the exit drive, they were old and isolated from the main park. It was decided to relocate many of the species to a shaded corner of woodland, where dappled light would form a tranquil backdrop for the pheasants. The five new aviaries were designed and built by the keepers in their spare time, so it was a while before construction was completed. Nevertheless, the first birds inhabited their enclosures by March. Quiet and sheltered, the area was perhaps overlooked by many visitors, with the train proving more of a draw than the pheasants. Shortly after, the planting around the station was enhanced, aided by the neutral pH of the heavy soil. *Tetrapanax papyrifera*, a fast-growing evergreen shrub with deeply cut leaves, quickly became established, along with many Chilean shrubs, including *chrinodendron*, *drimys* and *embothrium.* The most interesting plant, however, was the *dracunculus vulgaris* , which releases a pungent smell of rotting meat to attract pollinating flies.

Retirement of John Stone

August 2005 proved to be the end of an era for the Park with the retirement of John Stone, who had run the insect and butterfly exhibits since 1975. His many successes during those 30 years included the breeding of thousands of butterflies and the nurturing of some of the largest leaf-cutting ant colonies in the world. He confessed that he felt apprehensive about the future but also believed it was time to enjoy a non-working life. He left with many fond memories and enjoyed revisiting the Park as often as he could.[121]

With John's departure, the Insect House reverted to the Park's full control and was brought into the herpetology department. Several changes were made to the general layout in 2006, as the shop that had supplemented John's income was no longer required. An exit door was installed at the far end of the building, allowing for an improved one-way visitor flow, and more space was made available for exhibits. The ageing butterfly flight cage was treated to necessary redesign, extension and refurbishment. Finally, the keepers sought a solution to a worrying problem of escaping leaf-cutting ants. A gentle pump was installed into the tanks underneath the insects' elevated walkways, ensuring the circulating water would prevent bridges being created from dead leaf matter. The Park certainly missed John's extensive knowledge but necessity made the new guardians of the Insect House quick learners.

Completely new and ambitious animal exhibits were also planned. From 2004, a wide revamp of the walk-through lake area was under way. White-lipped peccaries, looking similar to small, hairy pigs, became the new neighbours of the tapirs and capybaras, which were mixed together in one exhibit. Chilean pudu, one of the world's smallest deer, and Parma wallabies were introduced in 2005. A further wooded area screened by evergreen trees was identified as an ideal space for extension. Canadian timber wolves were chosen as appropriate inhabitants and, at the beginning of 2006, work was begun on a new enclosure among the woodland beyond the flamingo lake. Although pet dogs had been welcome with visitors from 1970, the wolves were the first non-domesticated canine species to be kept at the Park. An elevated wooden walkway was constructed along one side of the perimeter fence, ensuring the animals could be seen anywhere in the enclosure. After months of building and preparation, four female wolves arrived in August 2006 from Longleat Safari Park, Wiltshire. Although the pack was initially quiet and unresponsive, they gradually settled in as the keepers proved to be innovative in their environmental enrichment ideas. The wolves particularly enjoyed sniffing and rolling around in the mounds of rhino dung transferred to their enclosure, as well as playing with the fleeces of recently sheared Ouessant sheep from the Children's Farmyard.

Madagascar

The introduction of new exhibits to the Park was heavily influenced by enthusiastic keepers. The impressive Madagascar project proved to be the prime example, as the brainchild of Jamie Craig. Jamie loved the variety and freedom offered by his workplace, encouraged by the trust and support of the Heyworths. His creativity was also stimulated by the fact that part of his new jurisdiction, the Walled Garden, was already undergoing some changes upon his arrival. As the giant hornbill enclosure was being enlarged, Tim Miles was improving its surroundings by redeveloping the north-west quadrant. Two pools of water were intersected by a wooden bridge, with koi carp on one side and beautiful lilies on the other. The space was large enough for the popular giant Amazonian water lily to be grown outdoors for the first time. The path exiting the Tropical House was re-routed among tall tree ferns and bamboo, guiding visitors past the colourful weaver birds and their intricate nests, woven from grasses and hung from the ceiling of their enclosure.[122] It was the rare Alaotran gentle lemurs found beyond this exhibit, however, which helped inspire the innovative Madagascar enclosure.

Lemurs were one of Jamie's favourite animals. They were characterful, did very well in captivity and were enjoyed by the public. When Dave Edgington asked for ideas for developing the original Pets' Corner, now just an area of under-used land just outside the Walled Garden and on the edge of the car park, Jamie knew immediately that lemurs should be the focus. He envisaged a large walkthrough exhibit, where visitors could immerse themselves in the sights, sounds and species of isolated Madagascar. He sketched some basic plans and submitted a proposal for the Heyworths to consider, then was amazed when the green light was given the following day.[123] As the initial advocate, Jamie was pleased to find that he was expected to shoulder responsibility for the project and would not be supervised by a bureaucratic committee, as in other zoos. No expensive professional consultants were required – Jamie and Tim Miles co-ordinated the entire project from some rough sketches.[124] Together, the section head and the head gardener liaised with the maintenance department and contractors to ensure that the concept was properly realised. Fortunately, Matthew Dix the steel fabricator from local firm Frank Fletcher and Sons was excellent at working without a design and constructed a tall frame for the exhibit with a tented roof of netting.[125] The gardens team then set to work remodelling the area, using the spoil from the foundations to create interesting, undulating terrain. Over the many months of development, ambitious ideas were frequently generated then discarded or integrated, ensuring the vibrant and organic growth of the project.

After an overall cost of £250,000, the new walkthrough exhibit was ready for its preliminary opening in October 2007. As soon as visitors entered, they were transported to a Madagascan island paradise. Many of the established trees and shrubs had been preserved, including several ornamental cherries. Among these, several tough species of palm and bamboo were planted to create a verdant, exotic environment.[126] Black and white ruffed, ring-tailed, collared and black lemurs all roamed freely, settling high in the trees or scampering across the paths. The mixing of these species enhanced their experience, encouraging more natural behaviour through the stimulation of interaction with other groups. The animals quickly worked out a hierarchy and learnt who and what to avoid. The landscape opened up as visitors followed the winding path through the exhibit, with a waterfall flowing into a large pool at the centre. This was occupied by black crowned night herons, purple swamp hens and Madagascan teal, while tortoises ambled nearby. Although the exhibit was generally open, two of the rarest primate species were kept in large enclosures bordering the area. The crowned sifakas and Alaotran gentle lemurs were simply so endangered that they required an additional level of protection. The resounding success of the new exhibit meant the official opening by Ruby Wax on 5 April 2008 was a proud moment for all involved.

This exhibit also embodied the ethos surrounding the Park's growing conservation efforts. Funds from visitor donations were used to aid some of the most critically endangered lemur species in Madagascar. An area of forest threatened by a mining company was protected for the crowned sifakas and contributions were made to a research programme surveying the location of greater bamboo lemurs in the wild.[127] Another long-term project funded by the Park involved work with the Tusk Trust charity, vaccinating domestic dogs in the Serengeti against rabies to prevent the disease being passed to local wildlife. Financial support was concentrated on a small number of projects that were close to the Park's heart, ensuring the impact of their contributions was not diluted.[128] Informing visitors of the Park's role in conservation was focused on raising awareness about endangered species generally. This was certainly achieved by the Madagascar walkthrough exhibit, educating through a close experience with creatures of the island.

After six productive years breathing new life into the Park, Dave Edgington retired in 2008 and moved to Lanzarote. His intelligence, creativity and energy meant he was a hard act to follow yet Jamie Craig appeared to be a natural successor. He continued Dave's open and accessible management style, relatively free from bureaucracy, which made the Park unusual among zoos. As the people most knowledgeable about the animals, the keepers were urged to put forward ideas for their workplace's running and development. Any suggestion, however, had to be well-planned and considered. If the plan was sound and the keeper was willing to take responsibility for its implementation, the management was willing to support them as far as possible. Such a process drew on everybody's experience and

Jamie Craig: curator, 2008-

Jamie had first started working with animals at the dolphinarium in Brighton at the age of 16 but joined the zoo-keeping profession later than most, due to a lack of job opportunities. He soon made up for lost time, however, gaining considerable experience and rising up the ranks at Drusilla's Zoo Park in Sussex from 1994 to 2002. Briefly involved in a speculative project seeking to establish a zoo in Portugal, he recognised the inherent instability of the scheme and returned to England. Jamie continued his career at Howletts Wild Animal Park in Kent then worked at Blackpool Zoo for three years, before considering another move in 2006. On seeing a position advertised at Cotswold Wildlife Park, he jumped at the opportunity, having enjoyed many visits to the place. He preferred it to a better paid job at London Zoo, because he was attracted by the lifestyle and "family atmosphere", which suited his wife and young children.[130] *He believed it was well-respected and professional but managed to retain the intimate, unique charm that made it so successful. In June 2006, therefore, he took up the position as head of the Walled Garden section and immediately unleashed a wealth of ideas and skill.*

The Madagascar project confirmed his talents and he worked closely with Dave, volunteering as assistant curator from 2007. He introduced a number of changes in this role, such as reorganising the staff sections of the Park from geographical areas to animal categories: birds, primates and small mammals, large mammals, and reptiles. He enjoyed excellent professional relationships with Reggie and John Heyworth but, crucially, had the knowledge and proven experience required for success as curator. After a short transitional period, therefore, he was promoted to the top job. There was no such thing as a typical day but the role could be summarised as oversight, management... and paperwork. Jamie arrives early in the morning to walk around the Park and chat to colleagues while it is quiet. All the mundane but necessary administration is then completed before tackling any recent issues or projects. The curator acts as a link between the sections to ensure that everything is running smoothly. Jamie thrives on this responsibility and feels privileged to be paid for doing something that he loves.

energy, relieving pressure on the managers and ensuring staff felt that they had made a real impact.[129] As with any workplace, discipline had to be maintained and tensions would occasionally arise, but a number of techniques were implemented to reduce any problems. Staff appraisals improved communication between keepers and their bosses, which ensured that changes were properly explained and any problems addressed. Regular keeper meetings after work performed a similar function and were conducted as an open forum, allowing staff to air grievances, raise issues and ask questions.[131]

As part of the Park's open management, all members of staff were encouraged to submit environmental enrichment ideas for the animals. This even included small competitions, with prizes for the best concept. Enrichment is an essential part of animal husbandry in modern zoos, providing for their physical and psychological well-being. Keepers work hard to invent species-specific means of stimulating natural behaviour to enhance a captive life. These are highly beneficial for any reasonably intelligent animals and also increase interest for the visitor. Enrichment can be as simple as keeping social animals in a social group or as complicated as training macaws to perform flying demonstrations.[132] Sensory enrichment is important and even mild negative stress can be useful, teaching animals to be alert and wary of potential predators. The most innovative methods are often food-based and the keepers enjoyed coming up with fun feeding techniques. The otters, for example, received an ice block containing a trout about once a month. They enjoyed clambering around on it in the water, before tearing the fish out in pieces as the ice started to melt. Some of the best enrichment activities involve everyday objects. For the red-handed tamarins, a cardboard tube from kitchen roll was filled with a few crickets, punctured with holes and the ends folded over. The monkeys then spent hours figuring out how to get at the treats inside.

Research programmes

Research is another key part of animal husbandry at the Park. Alongside the daily duties of cleaning and feeding the animals, the keepers also spend a significant amount of time observing and recording their behaviour. They develop a deep understanding of the various species, allowing any abnormal activity that suggests health problems to be spotted swiftly. Such study also allows keepers to consider changes to the environment which might improve an animal's general well-being or breeding record. If possible, significant findings are submitted in articles for animal husbandry journals, ensuring that the Park is part of a wide information network sharing good techniques and practices. Undergraduate students are also welcomed to conduct their research projects at the Park, with full access to the extensive knowledge of the keepers, in the hope that their conclusions will prove useful in the future.

All these investigations help the Wildlife Park fulfil its obligations to the wider zoo community. Genetic diversity must be maintained in captive populations, requiring constant communication over husbandry, health and breeding. This is facilitated by the compilers of stud books, who monitor a particular species and provide advice to institutions. The Park is also involved in several European endangered species programmes, the highest degree of species management, which requires signing up to a certain set of recommendations established by the species co-ordinator. Despite the Park's relatively small size, active involvement in these networks magnifies its reputation and ensures the greatest standard of living for its animals.

As well as being knowledgeable and good observers, keepers have to interact well with the public. As they carry out their work, they are required to be polite, friendly and prepared to talk to visitors. Although keepers are most commonly used as talking signposts, they enjoy talking about the animals they care for. Two new initiatives from the end of this decade greatly increased public engagement. First, the Animal Encounters scheme gave visitors the opportunity to learn more about the work of the keepers, while getting some hands-on experience with the animals. Lasting about half an hour, paying participants could choose from a variety of species to meet and feed, including the giant tortoises, penguins, lemurs, tapirs and capybaras.

The Keeper for a Day programme, however, was even more popular. First trialled by Jamie Craig and section head Mark Godwin in 2007, it offered people the opportunity to go behind the scenes.[133] This was an individual experience, with the visitor spending an entire day working one-on-one with a keeper across the whole scope of the

Park, involved in every aspect from feeding and enrichment activities to mucking the animals out. The programme was fully implemented in 2008, with a proportion of the funds raised going directly to conservation or keeper development projects.

This was important because a lot of money was being invested in improving the Park through various renovations. Starting in September 2007, Iri Gill, the new head of herpetology, oversaw the extensive refurbishment of the Reptile House. The building was old and a lot of the off-show facilities needed urgent modernisation. Finally completed in Spring 2008, newly installed displays replicated the natural environments for individual species from barren deserts and rocky waterfalls to tropical rainforests and freshwater pools. Mandy Palmer, normally part of the gardens department, was drafted in to create many of the woodland scenes with paint, logs and artificial leaves.[134] In her beautifully-decorated exhibits, deadly Gaboon vipers, Jamaican boas and poison arrow frogs were accommodated, among many other rare and fascinating reptiles.

Another important refurbishment was undertaken between January and March 2010, as the penguin enclosure and filtration system in the Walled Garden was completely overhauled. Its beach area was given a makeover to look like the Atacama coast of South America, which was ideal for the resident Humboldt penguins. Alongside the new exhibits introduced during a busy decade of development, improvements such as this were vital. Both Jamie and Reggie believed that the Park should be changing a little all the time, upholding high standards, keeping visitors interested and preventing stagnation. This principle was admirably upheld throughout the recession that rocked the world from 2008. Fortunately, visitor numbers were not as badly affected as they had been by the recession of the early 1990s, but a lot of work was required to keep the figures at a consistent level.

Old fittings could be renovated but, sadly, animals could not and over time several well-loved but elderly animal characters passed away. Gertie, the brown-haired spider monkey, was popular from the Park's opening day, initially living in an enclosure in the Walled Garden. She lived happily with her family for many years until the group was due to retire to Reeseheath College, near Chester, in March 2008. On the day of the move, however, age-related illnesses had left her very weak and the emotional decision was taken to put her to sleep. Jessei, the male Amur leopard, was also lost to extreme old age in February 2010. He had arrived a lot later than Gertie, in 2000, but quickly became a firm favourite. At the age of 18, he was probably the oldest of his species in the world, thanks to the care and attention he received. Finally, the Park's three original rhinos succumbed to age in this decade. Bella was the first to go, in 2003, followed by Paddy in 2007. In January 2010, the passing of the mild male, Bull, at the age of 42 was perhaps the loss most keenly felt; Reggie believed he would never know or love another animal as much as this gentle giant.[135] The rhino trio had been an essential fixture at the Park since 1972, grazing their paddock against the backdrop of the Manor House and English countryside. The deaths of all these animals were upsetting but keepers and visitors alike could treasure many happy memories of them.

New rhinos arrive

The arrival of young white rhinos, however, was symbolic of the generational transitions made throughout this decade. With the deaths of Bella and Paddy, plans had been established to bring in new females, with the hope of successfully breeding the species. In 2008, the existing house was renovated and extended, providing all the space required for mothers and their young. Bearing in mind that Bull would not last forever, boisterous Monty was brought in from his birthplace in Knowsley Safari Park in April 2009, given by the Earl of Derby. He was joined in his paddock by two females in November. With no suitable animals available in the zoo community, the Park had needed to look further afield.

The ideal candidates were found at Mafunyane Game Farm in South Africa, where the population had outgrown the holding capacity. In June 2009, Jamie Craig flew out to where the two rhinos were held in designated quarantine quarters, in order to check their health and finalise the transfer. The whole process actually took around four years, with long periods of frustrating uncertainty and bureaucracy delaying matters, to such an extent that Reggie wrote to the local MP (and future prime minister) David Cameron for help to force open the bureaucratic log-jam. Already by then leader of the Conservative Party, Cameron's willingness to raise the issue in the

House of Commons quickly cleared the way with the relevant ministry. It was all worth it to have a 'crash' of rhinos wandering the grounds of Bradwell Grove once again and the two new females were named Ruby (in anticipation of the Park's 40th anniversary) and Nancy, after David Cameron's daughter.

The 40th anniversary... with giraffes

As the Park edged towards its 40th anniversary, plans were afoot for its largest animal project to date. Giraffes were a favourite animal of John Heyworth and it had been his long-held ambition to include them in his Wildlife Park, but circumstances always intervened. In 2007, however, preliminary considerations and planning were begun under Dave Edgington. The right location had to be found, so that the required accommodation could be built without spoiling the landscape, and then the entire project had to be financed.[136] It was only when Jamie Craig became curator that real progress could be made. From the first site meeting in May 2009, work began in earnest and evolved from the original thinking. In a departure from some past experiences, the giraffe enclosure was a textbook example of how to manage a project.[137] Regular meetings ensured every angle was considered, progress was closely supervised and constant communication ensured each task was completed on schedule.

Construction began just before Christmas and, as with the Madagascar walkthrough, the skill of the team of local contractors under Andy Millard and Pete Benfield meant Jamie and the keepers just had to explain their concept for it to be realised by the builders. The Park's electrical contractor, Alan Price, who was a key source of expertise and advice on all of the Park's building projects since 1996, researched and supervised the installation of a ground-source heating system for the huge structure. The airy giraffe house included an elevated walkway, allowing eye-level observation of the animals as they grazed on the leaves and branches provided. Visitors also had excellent views as the giraffes strolled around their large paddock, with their enclosure surrounded by unobtrusive wire fencing and a deep ha-ha. In June 2010, three young males bred in other British zoos, Koife, Century and Wallace, arrived and gradually settled into their new surroundings.

The timing was perfect, allowing these new arrivals to become the focal point of the 40th anniversary celebrations. This was a proud moment for John Heyworth, crowned by the realisation of his dream to have the world's tallest mammals striding in the Cotswold countryside. They emerged into their enclosure for the first time on 11th June, at a huge garden party arranged to celebrate both the Park's 40th anniversary and John and Susan's 60th wedding anniversary. After days of miserable rain, the weather improved and the evening of the gathering was warm and clear. Everyone from the Park and estate as well as family friends of the Heyworths were invited to celebrate the special occasion and it gave many faces from the past the opportunity to return. Eileen Manley, from the ticket office, enjoyed seeing the first curator, Brian Sinfield, again after many years.[138] Former secretary Mavis Coupar loved catching up with many old friends and said it felt just like going home.[139] Over 300 people of all ages and backgrounds spent the evening chatting and reminiscing on the terrace by the Manor House, as a West Indian steel band (always loved by John and Sue Heyworth) played in the background and the light slowly faded. All present shared a common feeling: an appreciation for and an involvement in the beauty and charm of John Heyworth's lifetime achievement, the Cotswold Wildlife Park.

Even as the past was being remembered, thoughts turned to the future. After the completion of every major project, such as the giraffe enclosure, it was always the intention to pause for a couple of years and consolidate. Nevertheless, plans are constantly abounding. Flagship developments are rare but improvements are constant, preventing any particular area from looking tired. As the Park entered its fifth decade, there were hopes to make better use of the quarantine buildings in the Manor House courtyard, completing the quadrangle of exhibits in that area. Speculative ideas for the complete transformation of the lake area were also being considered. Contemplating his vision for the area in 2021, Reggie hoped that the ethos of beautiful open space that integrated animals and horticulture would be maintained under the stewardship of the Heyworth family. Loved by those who work, live and visit there, the Wildlife Park will continue to be successful by sticking to the values that have upheld it throughout its rich history.

Chapter 8

"Without them this would never have been possible"

THE LIVES OF THE KEEPERS

An entry-level zoo keeper today must demonstrate a passionate enthusiasm for their chosen career, an impressive array of work experience placements and often an academic qualification in zoology or animal management. Those lucky enough to secure a position in the competitive environment can expect to practise a lot more than simple animal husbandry. They become part of an international community, involved in research, conservation projects and public education. Many can expect to become highly specialised and earn additional duties, such as managing the European stud book for the captive breeding of a particular species. The responsibilities of an animal keeper at Cotswold Wildlife Park have evolved considerably over its lifetime. There will, however, always be one constant factor: the unavoidable chore of muck shovelling.

Two brothers, Gerry and Will Manley, were among the first 'keepers' at the Wildlife Park, despite their young age. Living locally in Filkins, they heard about the exciting venture in 1969 and were encouraged by their mother Eileen to enquire about jobs, which they did by knocking on the Heyworths' front door. Behind schedule and desperate for labour, John Heyworth thus turned up at the Walled Garden and proudly handed over nine-year-old Will to his head gardener, announcing: "I've got some help for you, Scott." Enthusiastically doing any task demanded of them, the Manleys proved their commitment and were soon able to start working with the animals, their real interest. Like any brothers, they could easily antagonise each other, so Gerry was placed on bottom section while Will, two years younger, became a member of top section.[140]

Every weekend and holiday was spent at the Park, which became a second home for the Manley family. Even on Christmas Day, when most people were unwrapping presents or tucking into roast turkey, the boys would be feeding animals and cleaning out enclosures.

As Brian Sinfield described them, the Manley brothers were "extraordinary" and a "great asset".[141] They were "born animal men" who, despite their small size, worked "like Trojans". When the school term began and his two young helpers were forced to disappear, he would find himself with far more work than expected.[142] For Will, the curator was an influential and supportive figure in this formative period of his life. He was particularly grateful that the management always quietly ignored any time restrictions on employing children under 14. There was always a danger of an ignorant bureaucrat believing they were being exploited but, in reality, the situation was quite different. There was nowhere the boys would rather have been and they earned a decent amount of pocket money doing a job they loved. Throughout their adolescence, they had the opportunity to meet and mix with a wonderful array of personalities, while contributing to a project close to their interests.

"Fantastic cameraderie"

Although older than Will and Gerry, the other members of the early keeping staff were fairly young, generally in their early twenties. Most had experience working in other zoological collections and there were several eccentric characters. For example, an Australian called Pete Walters, the first reptile keeper, was fearless but also rather irresponsible with regard to health and safety. Will enjoyed the fun atmosphere he and other characters created, and felt it was a sad loss when they moved onto other jobs. The boys were clearly very much part of this social group, with "fantastic camaraderie" and banter among them. The keepers were very welcoming and did not treat them differently, mainly because they were punctual, got stuck in and never moaned about the chores they were given. Particularly in the months before the Park opened, and for several years afterwards, it was "all hands to the pump" with everyone having to make do with the limited resources available.[143] As today, the separate animal kitchens were the hubs of activity and created two distinct sections. With a small staff, however, roles were far less demarcated, with anyone helping out wherever and whenever their labour was required. Shifts had to be covered even without the relevant experience, enclosures had to be repaired and escaped animals caught. On busy days, animal keeping duties were postponed to help sell tickets, direct car parking and collect litter.

Will remembers doing a number of jobs which were more unusual than many of today's duties. Unpleasant tasks included clearing out the unreliable waste systems and removing the waste to a pit at the nearby abandoned aerodrome. At the same dump, he once spent an afternoon picking maggots off the corpse of an ostrich, gathering desperately needed live food for a new arrival.[144] More fun could be had chasing the people who were seen climbing over the boundary fences as they sought to dodge paying for entrance. There were surprisingly frequent displays of dishonesty like this in the more rebellious 1970s. The Manley brothers also enjoyed driving tractors and other vehicles on the estate, which they were able to do as young as 14. Finally, they became adept at wielding screwdrivers to break into cars, as families commonly locked their keys inside. In Will's view, zoo keeping was less organised and professional in the 1970s but always interesting and exciting.

Will was too young to remember romantic tensions but, like any close working community, rumours of liaisons abounded at the Park. Many relationships were fleeting and the aftermath occasionally created a hostile environment. Martyn Williams and Jenny White, however, were the Park's original Romeo and Juliet, finding love despite being separated by section. Both had started working as keepers in 1974 but Jenny was part of top section, rising to section head in early 1979 before marrying Martyn and retiring in 1980. In total, Martyn worked for 12 years at the Park, rising to head keeper under Colin Fountain. His many achievements included developing a successful hand-rearing technique for Humboldt penguins. It was a great loss when he found another post in February 1986 but he left with a reference which described him well. In it, John Heyworth wrote,

"Martyn is a good mixer who is liked by everyone but at the same time is a good leader and organiser, honest, hardworking and conscientious – there is no member of the staff of whom I have a higher opinion."[145] Martyn and Jenny made many lifelong friends during their time at the Park and it provided a significant part of their personal history. Fortunately, their tale was happier than Shakespeare's play and they are presently enjoying life together in France.

Welshman Barry Graves worked with Jenny on top section in the late 1970s. He had gained experience in many animal collections since he began his zoo career at Dudley ten years earlier. Sadly, a few of these workplaces were stereotypical concrete menageries of the older generation, with caged enclosures and poor conditions. Some keepers practised controlling their animals through fear and intimidation, rather than understanding and observation. Barry's experience at Cotswold Wildlife Park, therefore, was a welcome departure. He had first visited on a day out in 1976 and fell for the place immediately, admiring its open plan and relaxed, uncrowded environment. At this point, the Park's reputation was still not widespread but Barry wanted to work with many of the large animals included in the African Plains paddock. When the position of rhino keeper became available (after the incumbent eloped with his girlfriend), Barry seized the opportunity and applied. He began work on 6 March 1978, his diary revealing that this was a fine, sunny day and he spent his first morning searching for two escaped meerkats.[146] He remained for eight years, rather longer than he originally envisioned. At this time, many keepers were "nomadic', often moving on to find new opportunities at another collection after just a couple of years. The feeling of community found at the Park often persuaded restless people, such as Barry, to settle down and establish roots.

A typical day for Barry would involve starting at eight and ensuring the enclosures were all cleaned out by ten, ready for when the gates were first opened to visitors.[147] Once the animals were put out on exhibit, he joked, not a lot then happened until lunch at noon. A large part of the job was observing the animals and visitors, ensuring they were all behaving as expected. Other cleaning, personal projects and maintenance jobs could be completed throughout the middle of the day. Keepers were responsible for keeping the enclosures of their animals in good repair. They also helped build other structures, such as aviaries and fences, when possible. Around four in the afternoon, the long routine of animal feeding was begun, which obviously took a variable amount of time depending on the number of animals and their geographical spread. The shift would then finish at five, with a rota established for the late duty of locking up around the Park. For many years, there was no established closing time and visitors simply drifted out. If a keeper was unlucky enough to be responsible for lock-up on a fine summer's day, they could be hanging around until nine in the evening. This inevitably tried their patience and they resorted to giving stragglers dirty glares before eventually hurrying them along.[148]

Keepers did not get many days off. The fortnightly schedule expected six days' work in the first week, and five and a half days in the second, with overtime paid after 5.30pm. An hour was given for lunch and 15 minutes for tea breaks in the morning and afternoon. These times, however, were flexibly followed, to the occasional frustration of the management.

Simple hierarchy

There was a very simple official hierarchy in the 1970s and early 1980s, with John Heyworth and the curator at the top, supported by the two section heads and then the keepers on the bottom rung. Within this, however, a pecking order emerged based on experience. "Snotty-nosed kids" starting straight from school were not eased in gently but "guided in a rather oppressive way".[149] Barry Graves laughed as he remembered the treatment of young Bryan Taylor, who started in 1980. Fortunately, Bryan was not dissuaded and he became one of the longest serving animal keepers at the Park. The way to become accepted was to get stuck in and get your hands dirty, as the focus was very much on gaining practical knowledge. The importance of engaging and interacting with visitors had not been universally acknowledged, with many keepers still considering the public as a 'necessary evil'. If questions were asked, they would be answered politely and to the best of the keeper's ability, but talks to school groups were rare. Any efforts to establish co-ordinated educational efforts were seen as a distraction from the main priority of caring for the animals, rather than as an inherent part of the job.

Rod Lane provided an ideal example of keeper recruitment at this time. He arrived at the Park shortly after Barry in April 1978 but stayed for much longer, finally retiring in February 2011. Rod's early background was in gardening and forestry, having worked in the parks department of Coventry Council and the Forestry Commission. Zoo keeping was not necessarily a vocation and many people came into the job after another practical career. In Rod's case, it was a case of who you knew as much as what you knew. He had become friendly with the curator, John Coborn, and the reptile keeper, Don Reid, through the Association for the Study of Reptiles and Amphibians. Without any prior involvement in zoos, the existing familiarity helped make his interview relaxed and all but a formality. It was enthusiasm and attitude, rather than experience, which was valued in potential staff and John Coborn felt Rod had "the makings of a good keeper".[150] The vacancy, however, was for work with the large animals of top section. Rod happily took the position, reasoning he could keep reptiles at home but that was not possible with camels and zebras.

Rod's responsibilities from his first day, therefore, included llamas, Bactrian camels, a couple of raccoons, capybaras and a pair of ostrich, adding the zebras to his duties soon after. With the arrival of the Bengal tigers in 1980, he gave up the llamas to look after the rare big cats. Rod particularly remembered a couple of the more characterful camels. One was so friendly it would follow him around the enclosure and even try to get into the wheelbarrow he pushed. He once had to hand-feed a youngster and if the bottle of milk wasn't finished, this other camel would "glug it down like a professional". Another camel, a male called Stavros, was addicted to extra-strong mints and acted as his keeper's best mate for most of the year, but became dangerously temperamental when in rut. From Rod's perspective, the routine was always the same but every day was a little different, as it threw up unique situations. He found his niche and concluded, "If you find a job that you enjoy doing, you never have to work a day in your life."[151]

Rod Lane witnessed a necessary transformation in the increasing professionalism of the animal keeper job. He described the organisation when he first started as "a bit casual',[152] with a fairly lackadaisical approach to money, time-keeping and appearance. John Coborn had tried to increase discipline and Bob Golding began to improve public relations but it was a long and gradual process. Will Manley remembers a simple uniform, requiring shorts and a khaki shirt with a yellow Cotswold Wildlife Park badge sown on. These regulations, nevertheless, were frequently flouted and often a keeper could not be told apart from a badly dressed visitor. Public presentation became increasingly important and concerning for John Heyworth, who always wanted to give the impression of a hard-working, efficient staff. Keepers were instructed to walk around singly and not in groups. In a complaint to Colin Fountain in 1987, he simply noted, "Tea breaks rather too long – all keepers sitting on bench in full view."[153] A section heads meeting in January 1984 warned staff to "not strip off if working in front of the public". A standard issue uniform was introduced in the late 1980s but an irritated curator's memo shows many members of staff were still not wearing it properly by 1993. The struggle was finally won and, in 2010, all keepers were recognisable in their warm green jumpers, complete with embroidered zebra head logo.

Public education

The greatest improvements, however, were made in engaging with visitors and providing talks for public education. This became a prerequisite for all modern, responsible zoos. Clearly, there was a general expectation of behaviour and polite customer service. In earlier years, this was sometimes forgotten under pressure or in frustration. Colin and Maria Fountain remember a keeper in the 1970s going to feed the penguins but tripping in front of the large crowd. Embarrassed, he loudly used some "undiplomatic" language and simply dumped the fish in the pool before marching away from the shocked onlookers.[154] The penguin feeding, nevertheless, was among the first efforts to offer pleasing and informative presentations to an audience. Keepers were gradually persuaded to be more welcoming to visitors and became aware of the value of their increased public presence.

Simon Blackwell was a crucial figure in encouraging improved education services and greater public interaction.[155] At an early age, his father had passed on an interest in ornithology but he began his working life at a printing technology firm. Fortunately he soon decided to pursue a career in animal keeping and was first employed at the exotic bird collection at Leeds Castle in Kent before moving to Cotswold Wildlife Park in December 1977. Although he had only previously worked with birds, he was assigned to Pets' Corner to care for guinea pigs, rabbits and other small mammals. The first person he remembered meeting was John Simmons, the head of bottom section, who had been with the Park since 1972. He also worked closely with Martyn Williams who, with an additional two years' experience, was always one rung ahead of Simon on the career ladder. The two men were typical examples of the friendly, playful characters found at the Park. With his positive and outgoing personality, Simon quickly settled in. Close friendships and loyalty to the section were established from the beginning. Simon, however, was always seeking new challenges and his ambition did not go unnoticed. When Martyn left for Drusillas Zoo Park, Sussex in 1986, Simon was promoted to be the new head keeper. Only a couple of years later, he became assistant curator, a position he held until his departure in 1998 to become general manager of Birdland in Bourton-on-the-Water.

For Simon, animal keepers could generally be defined by two types. He was proactive in seeking out new experiences and opportunities, whereas others were capable but comfortable, happy to work in the same department of the same collection. During the 1980s, Simon felt the Park was blessed with many keepers of the former attitude. His colleagues were completely absorbed in the welfare of their animals and continually striving to learn more about them. Tea breaks would be spent sitting together reading zoology books and asking each other questions. He praised how the Park emphasised the importance of learning on the job, often introducing staff to work with completely unfamiliar animals. Barry and Simon arranged an informal two-month section exchange, whereby the two men traded their responsibilities to extend their knowledge. On the very first day, Barry walked into an aviary and stood helplessly as a yellow double-fronted Amazon parrot escaped over his shoulder and through the gaping door.[156] Although he was inevitably mocked by his peers, everybody recognised that a day was wasted if you hadn't learned something. Mistakes were all part of that process. A commitment to widening practical understanding was a crucial factor in ensuring the Park gained, and retained, a good reputation for animal husbandry and well-designed enclosures.

Colleagues can often make the difference between a working day being an endless chore or a pleasing experience. Simon Blackwell's enjoyment of the job was greatly enhanced by the people he worked with, partly explaining why he spent 21 years at the Park. In addition to sharing knowledge, there was a "silliness" and spontaneity among the keepers of bottom section, which he loved.[157] Dangerous pranks, such as locking people in freezers, were commonplace. Such antics are unlikely to gain approval as a modern team-building technique, but the playful spirit created strong bonds. Colin Fountain, however, was not always impressed with the rebellious nature of bottom section; aligned with top section and its larger, more unpredictable animals, safety and sensible practice were among his top priorities. An early personality clash between Colin and Simon, the self-described "party animal", intensified rivalry between the two sections but eventually a mutual respect developed for each other's work. Furthermore, increasing responsibility and professionalism in animal keeping meant staff could not mess around to the same reckless extent.

Health and safety

Although the lives of animal keepers necessarily involve danger, attention to health and safety has improved significantly. In the early years, Park staff were fortunate that the only serious injuries suffered were broken bones, as there are many stories of near-misses. Will Manley remembers that Brian Sinfield would be furious if people did not keep up to date with their tetanus vaccinations, but otherwise safety regulations were fairly non-existent. When helping clean out an enclosure in the Reptile House, Will almost broke through the glass window when he found a poisonous black moccasin snake had been placed in with him by Pete Walters. Another prank involved throwing car keys into the piranha tank of the aquarium. In the evening, keepers would frequently be alone in enclosures with large animals without any means of attracting attention if required. A small whistle was the only way of raising an alarm, before hand-held radios transformed keeper communications. However, only luck and quick thinking, not a radio, could help Mike Woolham survive an attack by an enraged male ostrich in the late 1990s. When he was putting it away one wet evening, the bird got loose and bore down upon him. To avoid the strong kicking legs and disembowelling talons, he had to throw himself down to the ground and suffer being stamped on until it stalked away. As a result, the story became a comical one of him stinking and caked in mud, rather than a tale of a nasty accident.[158]

When in close proximity to animals, it was vital that a keeper could dismiss all other concerns and focus entirely on their work. No matter how well staff thought they knew an individual creature, they always had to be recognised as unpredictable and capable of harm. During his long career, Colin Fountain encountered a number of close calls, where a lapse of concentration could create a dangerous situation. After a renovation of the Amur leopard enclosure, Colin was not happy with one of the barriers in the housing block. A keeper had been lightly scratched through a gap in it, so he requested that it was reinforced. Annoyed to discover that this had not been done, he stormed down to the enclosure with a tool kit to sort it out himself. He had been working for some time when a sheepish colleague turned up to apologise, and instead pointed out that the leopard was in the next partition with full access to Colin. It had been lying on a platform calmly watching the distracted curator and could easily have sprung across to bite his exposed neck.

Another occasion found Colin and Simon trying to feed antibiotic tablets to a 12-foot python. As Simon went to administer the medicine, the snake jerked from Colin's grip and bit down on his hand. The backwards-pointing teeth made the process of extracting it considerably more difficult, cutting his fingers deeply. He had to get his hand free quickly, however, because the snake had also begun throwing its body in coils around Colin, attempting to crush him. All the while, the visitors on the other side of the glass were watching in excited amazement, believing it was all a clever stunt.[159] Clearly, the very nature of the job means keepers are always going to court risk, no matter the precautionary regulations put in place. How they reflect on these situations gives an insight into the keepers' mentality. Without sarcasm, Simon Blackwell described the python experience as a "lovely story", while Colin and Maria Fountain laughed as they said the funniest memories mostly involved injury.

Capturing escapees was another activity frequently featuring in the early lives of animal keepers. When the Park opened for the first time, the exploits of a herd of sika deer stirred local attention. On a press day in March 1970, a group of journalists was being shown around the lake enclosure, which the sikas shared with cranes, flamingos and waterfowl. When the party was distracted, the deer managed to slip through the double set of gates and made a dash for freedom. Sightings of the animals in someone's garden or farmyard were reported to the Park over the next few months. This required the keepers to charge out with nets and crates but they always returned empty-handed. In the summer, a fawn was discovered and used as bait to try to catch its mother, but the animal's naturally nervous disposition caused this to fail. They were given up as a lost cause and were left to enjoy their liberty.

Animal escapes

From the very beginning, the Park's records were littered with notes of animal disappearances and escapes. In 1985, three speckled kingsnakes were on the loose, with one at large for five months until it was found in the neighbouring crocodile pool. The yellow mongoose arrived at the Park for the first time in December 1990. It seemed to settle well into its enclosure in the Walled Garden until, three months later, it succeeded in jumping the wall. Keepers needed to think creatively and come up with innovative solutions for recapture but a lot of chance was also involved. Barry Graves remembers how a flamingo, which had been helped over the fence by a fortuitous wind, was caught with the unusual help of John Heyworth's horse. Mr Heyworth was a keen rider and could commonly be seen enjoying a canter around his estate. Unfortunately for the flamingo, it had landed in the stallion's paddock and was herded into a corner until it was gratefully collected by the keepers.[160] The Heyworth family always held a reputation for their impeccably trained animals, but this example surpassed all expectations.

Once, a sturdy barrier was temporarily left open by the rhino house while Rod Lane and Barry Graves were feeding them. Instead of happily munching on the bales of hay provided, Paddy had wandered close to this opening and only a chain-link fence stood between her and the Oxfordshire countryside. Barry managed to draw her back to safety with a bucket full of nuts and some sweet talking. All zoos must have various plans to deal with the eventuality of an animal escape, depending on its size and threat to public safety. Animal capture teams are mobilised and non-keeper staff ordered to keep indoors. If a serious danger is posed, the firearms team is called out, comprising some members of staff and outside shooting experts. Clay pigeon shoots or static firing ranges provide the necessary regular practice with a range of different calibres. Mark Godwin, the current head of top section, enforces rigorous regulation on the keeping and use of these firearms. In the past, Colin Fountain and Simon Blackwell, as general manager and assistant curator, were predominantly responsible for the enacting of the safety protocol. Thankfully, however, the Park has never suffered any serious escapes by large animals necessitating such extreme action. The most harm Simon encountered in one of these situations was being dragged along the ground by a camel he had lassoed in the car park, as it raced back towards its enclosure.[161]

The working environment at the Park has generally been very open, with staff encouraged to offer their thoughts and become involved in projects that interest them. This became more apparent with the new generation of management inaugurated by Reggie Heyworth and Dave Edgington. To complement the section head meetings, Dave introduced keepers' meetings, whereby members of staff would get together one evening after work to discuss issues and concerns. Their input provided alternative perspectives and their opinions were recorded, helping employees feel valued even if no further action was taken.[162] Many new keepers were surprised to find themselves given more responsibility than expected but rose to the challenge. Compared to other collections, they worked with a greater variety of species and with closer contact on a daily basis. Teamwork and individual initiative were extremely important, with trust based on ability and not merely length of service.[163] Time and support were provided for staff to pursue personal interests in relation to their animals. Such close involvement helped them feel like they had an essential stake in the Park's success, inspiring enduring affection and loyalty.

The running of the Park by the Heyworths as a family business has been a crucial factor in maintaining this inclusive atmosphere. Although there was little concern about the intricacies of business and finance among the animal keepers, the consequences obviously had implications for them. For one, they could never forget the link between visitor numbers and the security of their jobs. Once the Park had become established, the general management was left to the curators but John Heyworth was kept well informed and would visit several times a week to check on everything. He was therefore familiar with his employees and they found him very approachable. Even if the pay was not particularly lucrative, they had an employer who knew them and was aware of their concerns. If the company had become a Trust, moreover, countless layers of formal bureaucracy and administrative costs would have been added. There was a danger that boards and committees would create obstacles and withdraw the initiative from individual members of staff. As a private family affair, personality and a sense of community was encouraged.

At the beginning of 1978, an article in the *Witney Gazette* concluded with a quotation from John Heyworth: "The success of this wildlife park... has depended more than anything else on the goodwill and team spirit of all those who work here. Without their help, and their dedication, none of this would ever have been possible."[164]

This opinion only grew stronger and John had tremendous respect for all of his staff. He was very proud of the expansion of the workforce to over 100 employees plus part-time helpers. Getting the right labour, he said, was always one of the most challenging aspects of managing the Park. Over the years, he appreciated meeting an extraordinary collection of characters dedicated to their jobs.[165] There was always a friendly relationship, but some distance necessarily remained. Throughout his career, for example, he was respectfully referred to as Mr Heyworth. He recognised, however, that the animal keepers were at the very heart of the Park's achievements. Their public presentation increased, their professionalism improved and their duties changed over the Park's history. The connection between employer and employees, nevertheless, ensured that mutual respect and loyalty were constants.

Chapter 9

"Planning the next generation's gardens"

GROUNDS, GARDENS & GARDENERS

When contemplating the future of Bradwell Grove Manor House in 1969, John Heyworth felt that the landscape was simply too beautiful to remain unseen and go to waste. From the beginning, therefore, the 120 acres of natural, open surroundings were crucial for creating the idyllic atmosphere which makes the site unique for so many visitors. Although it is now simply impossible to imagine Cotswold Wildlife Park without its picturesque gardens and flourishing grounds, creating and maintaining the setting required a lot of hard work. The task was made more challenging by the inhabitants of the aviaries and enclosures. Through integrating animals and plants, the keepers and gardeners necessarily formed a productive partnership, although clashes of interest frequently arose.

As head gardener for nearly 30 years, Les Scott was a major contributor to the Park, his involvement helping to sow the seeds of success. He was an instantly recognisable figure, small and slight with dark hair, always wearing dungarees and a green, woolly hat resting on the back of his head. He could often be found working in the potting shed or pruning plants in the Tropical House. With a fondness for mints, it was guaranteed that a bag of sticky sweets could be found in his pocket, covered in fluff and flecks of compost.

He would readily offer these dubious treats to his colleagues, a reflection of his genuine and generous character. Dedicated to his loving wife Lillian, whom he had married as a teenager, his boyish charm still made him a favourite among the ladies at the Park. Mavis Coupar, when she worked as a secretary, would often take her lunch in the Walled Garden to enjoy the flowers and was often teased by "cheeky" Les.[166] Described as a "real gardener and a real gentleman",[167] he is remembered with true affection by all.

After first meeting Les, John Heyworth thought he had possibly been a "trifle nervy" but was "obviously a good man in every way".[168] The gardens were to be completely separate from the jurisdiction of the curator, meaning Les was fiercely independent and reported directly to Mr Heyworth. This was clearly something the second curator, John Coborn, readily acknowledged, observing during a reorganisation of staff in 1979 that Les "would hate to be responsible to anyone else".[169] Despite the very different backgrounds of the head gardener and his employer, they established an effective working relationship. This was aided by their common botanical interest and dedication to the project. Lillian Scott described the partnership between the two men as "brilliant", because their minds were on the same track. Les, however, had to learn quickly not to ask for something until it was really needed, because John did things immediately. There was no point asking for turf to be ordered, for example, if it was not required for a couple of weeks, as it would be waiting the next day.[170] The Insect House keeper John Stone also remembered that they made a comical-looking pair as they walked around examining the Park, with little 'Scotty' needing to trot to keep up with the long stride of John Heyworth.[171]

"Fit as a fiddle" and tanned from a career working outdoors,[172] Les was a tireless worker with the necessary experience and commitment for his job. Thrift was another attribute he shared with his boss. This was essential considering the limited money available in the early years. Self-sufficiency was vital, as it was financially impossible to purchase everything on a growing list of planting demands. All the bedding plants for the Park were grown in three greenhouses at the end of the Walled Garden. The ageing Victorian structures were replaced towards the end of 1973, after rotting wood and loose glass made them too hazardous. Les eventually had to dedicate his own greenhouse at home to the growing of Park flora, as more and more specimens were required. In 1981, only £50 was spent on the plants required for the new Tropical House, as the majority were grown from donated cuttings. Although labour intensive, the practice has continued for more than 40 years, proving to be a cheap and efficient way of supplying much of the content required for flower beds and exhibits.

The Walled Garden

The Walled Garden was the main focus of Les Scott's early efforts and provided the best example of his style. Its transformation was the priority for opening day but it still took several years to become properly established. Previously a well-cultivated kitchen garden, the soil was of good quality but it has been badly compacted by the heavy construction machinery rolling over it as pools and enclosures were built. The 12-foot-high walls sheltered the area from high winds and kept rabbits away from young plants, but frost could also become trapped in shaded areas, raising all sorts of challenges in winter. Over time, however, plenty of top soil, compost and rhino dung was helping to produce well-ordered, colourful flower displays.

Once the layout and content of the Walled Garden had been established, there were few great changes in this area while Les was at the helm. The penguin pool, otters and waterfowl enclosure bordered the south wall, with square wooden aviaries running along the rest. Just in front of the Tropical House, a circular reptile pit lay between two more large aviaries. Wide paths wound between the three curved grass lawns, which took up most of the central area and encompassed the shaped flower beds. In his words, these beds followed a "formal design", to be complimented with shrubs and specimen trees scattered around their borders.[173] He intended an open environment which showed a wide variety of colourful plants, sensible for the climate and conditions. The result was a neat and organised display, similar to the town corporation style that Les had learned during his time working with the Weymouth parks department. It was not exotic or spectacular, but it was appropriate for the time and setting. Visually pleasing and comfortable, the appeal to visitors was increased by the obvious labour of love shown by the gardens department. Great planning was required for the bedding plants, grown on an impressive scale and to a strict schedule.

Even if a spring border still looked thriving and attractive, everything was pulled out at a set date to be replaced by the summer flowers.

In the wider grounds, Les said he could only hope to complement the "inherited beauty of the many fine trees and landscape".[174] The Park benefited enormously from its array of trees, with mature species of beech, yew, ash, cedar, chestnut and others to be found. Many had been introduced by William Hervey, the original 19th century owner of the Manor House. John Heyworth felt passionately about preserving their presence and more than 300,000 trees have been planted over the estate since he inherited it in 1949. The tallest tree in the Park, indeed for many miles around, was a 130-foot *wellingtonia*, about 160 years old, but this could still be considered a sapling compared to the ancient gnarled oak by the restaurant, reckoned to be more than 600 years old.

Whenever any development work was started, a great deal of consideration was required before action involving established trees was taken. If any were felled, it was predominantly due to their dangerous condition caused by extreme old age, weather or diseases, such as those which devastated the elm and sycamore populations in the late 1970s. Even then, the remains were put to good use. In 1990, for example, a huge crane was hired to lower a cypress, brought down by a gale, into the spider monkey enclosure. The creators of the Park ensured trees and their fruit were compatible with the animals but used every opportunity to integrate exhibits with the existing landscape.

Another gardening legacy was created in 1989 with the transformation of the south terrace of the Manor House. Daisy Louisa Eley, a regular admiring visitor but unknown to the staff, bequeathed £32,500 to the Park in her will. It was decided that £10,000 would be spent on a formal space to commemorate her and thank her generosity. Unlike the winding paths of the Walled Garden, this was to be a parterre, a patterned symmetrical memorial garden. A stone balustrade ran along the terrace, with steps on either side of a raised lily pond leading down to the lawn level. A *magnolia grandiflora* was trained against the house wall and produced large, creamy, scented flowers in the summer and early autumn. Alongside this also grew *wisteria* , until it began causing damage to the lead drainpipes and was mostly removed in 2000. Central box-edged beds were introduced, with forget-me-nots planted in spring and white *argyranthemum* and purple *heliotropium* in summer. Around the outer beds, *petunia* and *acidanthera* bloomed. In this particularly public area between the bar and the brass rubbing room, the terrace harmonised with the architectural style of the house and demonstrated the ornamental skill of the gardeners.

The garden shop

In the opening season of 1970, many admiring visitors made enquiries about the plants for their own gardens. This presented an unexpected commercial opportunity for the gardens department. With his boss's permission, Les and his wife began a weekend stall selling popular plants, such as *fuchsia* and *begonia* , and received 30% of the profits. John Heyworth, always aware of the need to increase revenue, began to investigate the idea of establishing a proper garden centre. Compensating Les for any loss of income by a wage increase, he decided to retain control of a specially constructed building and its site, while the business would be sourced to an outside company. A garden shop along the outside south wall of the Walled Garden was proposed, separated from the car park by an existing ha-ha. Planning permission was granted on 27 January 1971. During protracted negotiations with Great Gardens of England Ltd, an agreement was signed in July 1971 stating that the company would hold responsibility for the building and staff, paying Mr Heyworth 10% of turnover and allowing any of the Park's surplus plants to be sold in the garden centre on its behalf. The contract was initially signed for 14 years, but the venture proved to be a disappointment for both parties, with consequently fraught relations. Fluctuating visitor numbers throughout the year meant Great Gardens of England barely broke even and the Park management felt that the company was failing to maintain its area properly. A clause in the contract to break the partnership was thus used in 1973 and the building reverted to Heyworth's control.

This space subsequently became a more modest garden shop, which was run with impressive efficiency by a Park employee called Margaret Mitchell. She lived in Burford and was hired for her experience of retail and customer service, having worked for John Lewis stores. Coming from a military family, she was apparently a "splendid" woman but also described as "formidable".[175] She clearly knew her own mind and how to get what she wanted, which did not always suit younger staff. She got on very well with Susan Heyworth, who wanted the opportunity to become more involved in the Park and had previously tried helping in the gift shop. She admitted that this was unsuccessful and all her selections were left on the shelf, as she had no idea what products the public wanted to buy. She was particularly interested in gardening, however, and these talents were put to more effective and enjoyable use when choosing flowers for sale. She loved getting up at four in the morning to journey with Mrs Mitchell to Covent Garden market in London, where they would load up their trailer with flowers and bedding plants to be sold back at the Park.[176] Pretty and popular, the garden shop carried along adequately but was not especially profitable. This was not helped when visitors, alone in the car park at the end of the day, would pilfer a couple of plant boxes and drive off.[177] At the end of the 1985 summer season, Mrs Mitchell retired and her shop was converted to sell children's toys.

By the late 1990s, health issues required Les Scott to slow down and eventually forced him to retire. He relinquished his position as head gardener in 1998, aged 75, but continued to work part-time for another year. During his long, dedicated service, he could not see his job as work because he enjoyed it so much. Although rarely taking a holiday, he had once toured Europe with his family and returned to places where he had fought as a young man in the Second World War. Aged just 18, he had been drafted into the Royal Engineers in May 1941 and saw action in Sicily, Italy and Austria. Although he could never forget that time, he would rarely talk about it. He was, however, able to find peace in the gardens of Cotswold Wildlife Park. Throughout his horticultural career, he treasured a passage by Reverend Samuel Hole (1819-1904), a clergyman and amateur gardener who founded the National Rose Society: "In all gardens, and in all gardeners, we find a home and brothers."

Dean Hole's words resonated with Les because he treasured the home he found at the Park and the brothers among his colleagues. When he died aged 83 in March 2006, his family found comfort in the knowledge that the Wildlife Park had been his paradise, his heaven on earth, a place he never wanted to leave and a place where

This aerial photo shows just a fraction of the Park, with the Manor House and its courtyard behind at the top, and rhinos on the African Plains in the centre

The evolution of the Tropical House is typical of the ongoing development work at the Park. In 1971 (top) it was first created by adapting a row of greenhouses in the Walled Garden. A decade later this was dismantled and completely rebuilt (centre), with a higher roof allowing a wider variety of tropical flora to be planted. In 2004 this was re-glazed and redesigned – the pictures at the bottom show the transformation

The keepers at the Park have always enjoyed great cameraderie, and a wide variety of tasks to perform. Gerry and Will Manley, pictured below, started working for the Park as small boys and soon became an indispensable part of the team

Animal husbandry is a vital part of the Park's work behind the scenes.
Above, rearing penguins. Below, an Amur leopard has a cataract operation

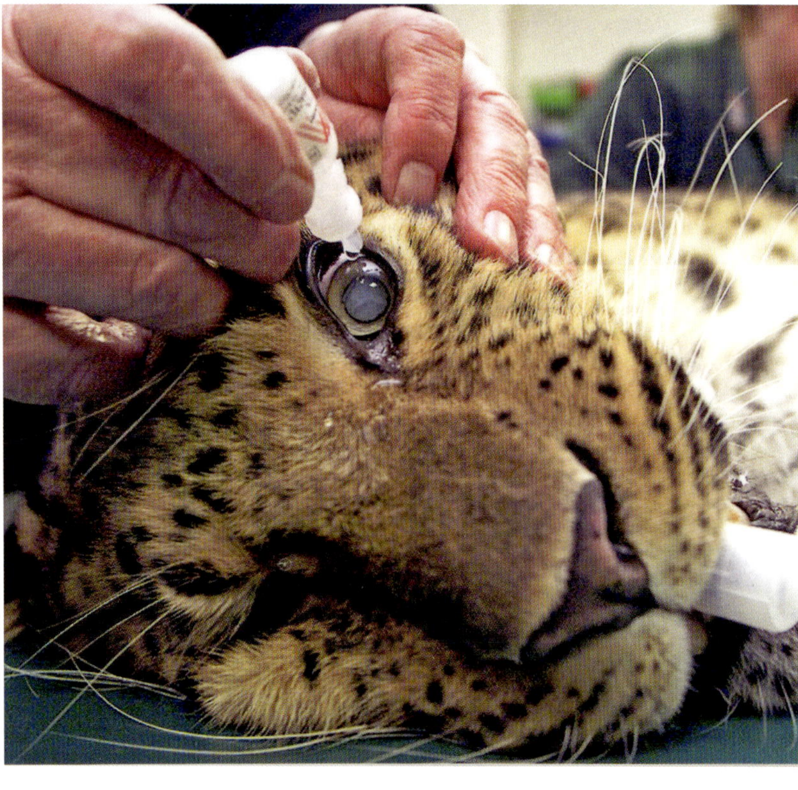

The gardens are central to the Park's appeal. Left, Les Scott was the Park's first head gardener and held the post for nearly 30 years. Above right, his original team of George Pitelen and Sid Simpson, both retired employees of the Bradwell Grove estate.
Below, the gardening team is now headed by Tim Miles (centre front)

The Park has long provided a variety of family entertainments beyond the animals and gardens. Top, donkey rides were popular in the 1970s and 1980s. Centre, the miniature railway first opened in 1974. Bottom, an adventure playground was a feature from the beginning

With many staff living on site, there is a strong sense of community at the Park. This is helped by regular social events. Above, a garden party hosted by the Heyworths in 1986 (John Heyworth is pictured far right). Below, the Park's band 'Jinxed' at a staff fancy dress party – former curator Dave Edgington is pictured at the left on guitar

Staff photos from the 1970s and 2009 show how the Park has grown over four decades

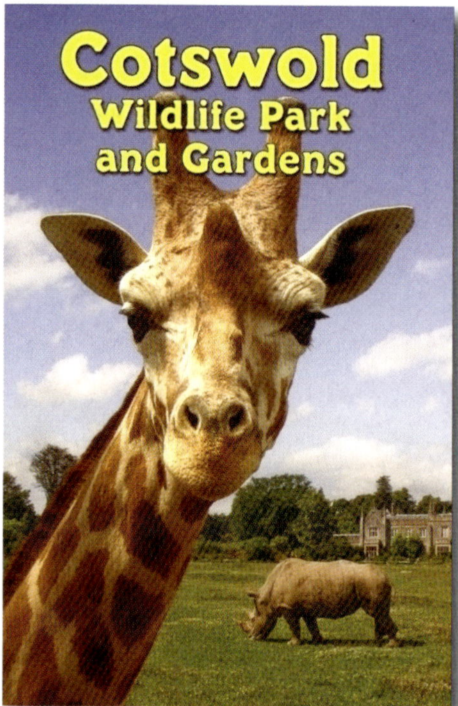

The changing face of the Park's guidebooks and newsletters between 1970 and 2012

Cotswold Wildlife Park & Gardens WILD TALK 2012

'LIVE 'n' DEADLY' from the Park

Debbie Ryan organised the BBC's flagship children's television show 'Live 'n' Deadly' to broadcast live from the Park on 5th November 2011.

The show kicked off with hosts Steve Backshall and Naomi Wilkinson measuring Barney, the Park's longest snake. This was no mean feat considering Barney is over twenty four feet in length and doesn't stay still for a second. It took six people in total to hold Barney for the task!

. . . one of the weirdest animals on earth . . .

Steve and Naomi got up close to many of the Park's animals including; the Wolverines, Crocodiles, Tapirs and the world's largest rodent, the Capybara. Steve delighted viewers with a close-up of the Gant Anteaters, which he described as "one of the weirdest animals on earth" with a tongue to match! Live from inside the Bat House, Steve answered viewers' questions while fifty Egyptian fruit bats flew around him. Naomi featured Red Panda *Doodo* in the 'Dead Cute' section of the show (pictured with keeper Bryan Taylor), which she said was one of her favourites. Steve's favourite animal also played a starring role as he joined the pack of wolves inside their enclosure.

BAFTA award winner 2011 (for best presenter) Steve said:

'We had a totally crazy time at Cotswold Wildlife Park. Going claw-to-claw with a giant anteater was a particular highlight and you have the biggest snake I've ever seen... and that's saying something!'

After the show, Steve and Naomi met the children from Brize Norton Primary School for a photo and signing session, which delighted their fans and Barney the reticulated python was voted the 'Ultimate Deadliest' animal of the show.

Burford, Oxford OX18 4JP Telephone: 01993 823006

The Park relies on publicity – some of it deliberate, such as the annual measuring of the Park's longest snake, and some unplanned: the image of the zebra chasing a rhino reached the tabloid newspapers. Below, in 2007 a six-part documentary, *Park Life*, gave the public a view behind the scenes

Celebrities have often helped attract interest in the Park. Above, Chris Tarrant with insect keeper John Stone on *Tiswas* in the late 1970s. Below, Johnny Morris and Cocky the cockatoo, a resident of the Park, stars of *Animal Magic*, which ran until 1983

Above: Ruby Wax was on hand for the launch of the Madagascar walkthrough enclosure in 2007. Below: Michaela Strachan filmed Zoo Babies for Channel Five at the Park in 2008. She is pictured with current curator Jamie Craig

A gift shop has always been a feature of the Park, particularly attractive to younger visitors. In 2011 a new, expanded shop was opened by Susan Heyworth

The Park showcases a wide variety of animals. From top: a Humboldt penguin; ruffed lemurs; an African leopard; giant tortoises young and old; and a red-bellied tamarin

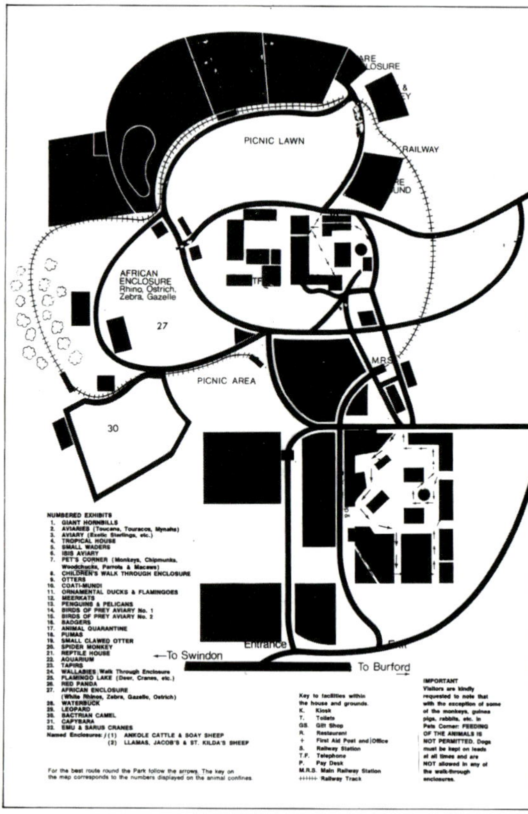

Maps of the Park show just how much has changed over 40 years. The plan above, from 1975, shows the recent addition of the African Plains. Below is the Park in 2012

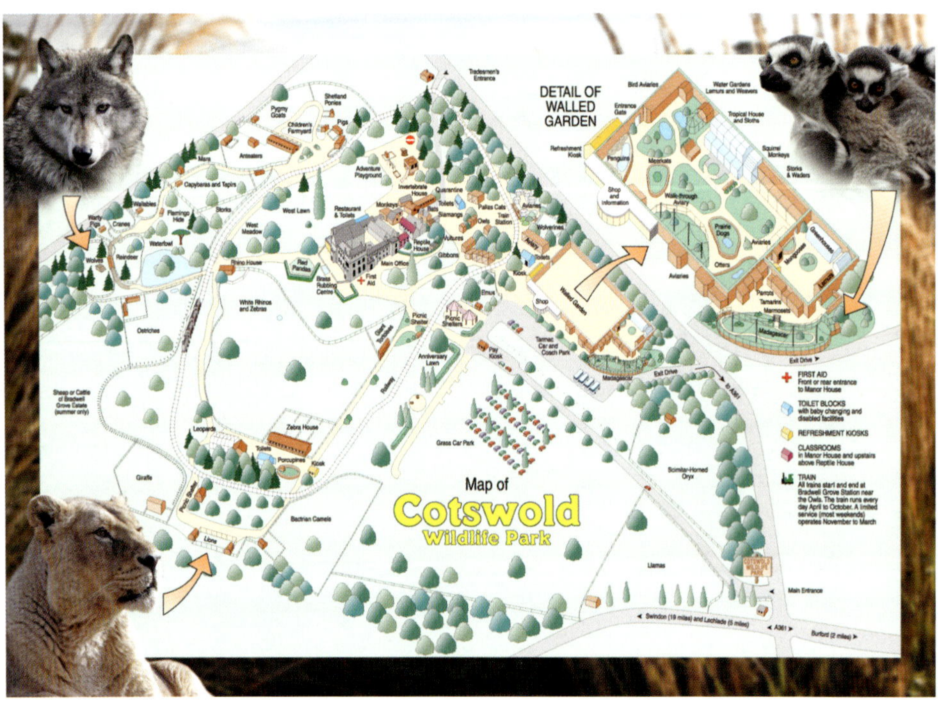

he truly belonged.[178] A simple plaque and a weeping golden beech tree commemorate him in the wooded lake area.

A new head gardener

Les's successor as head gardener was a very different character. Tim Miles was a tall, slim man with an outgoing personality and a lot of ambition. Growing up in Cornwall, his father's keen gardening fostered his own interest from an early age. The mild and sunny climate also meant that he was exposed to an array of exotic-looking plants. This was consequently a style that he always sought to export to the places he worked. After training at Cannington College, Somerset, his first job in a wide-ranging career was as a gardener and presenter for BBC Plymouth, which offered him a first tantalising taste of showmanship. Between 1982 and 1989, Tim then worked as head gardener for the Peper Harow therapeutic community in Surrey. The aim was to provide lush, natural surroundings to help adolescents with mental health problems from disadvantaged backgrounds. Following that, two and a half years spent at London Zoo provided experience combining horticulture with zoo exhibits, which was still a relatively unknown practice in Britain at the time. From 1992, he worked on a private estate in Hampshire before briefly returning to Cornwall as curator for the Lost Gardens of Heligan. When offered the head gardener's role at the Wildlife Park, he was delighted by the opportunity and began his new job on 1 June 1998.

John Heyworth had tremendous respect for Les Scott's committed work but, by the time he retired, felt the look had remained static for too long. The Walled Garden in particular was pretty but dated. He was very aware that garden visiting had become a greater commercial opportunity, as people were living longer, retiring earlier and were more readily spending the 'grey pound'. John and Reggie Heyworth were therefore keen to maximise the potential of the grounds as an attraction in their own right. With few personal preconceptions about what this entailed, they wanted someone with the ideas and energy to bring about this transformation, for which they concluded that Tim was the ideal man, although they did not expect the transition to be a smooth one. Tim himself described his gardening attitude as a paradox, meaning he worked in a tranquil setting but was personally driven by the excitement of creating something for an audience.[179] His early days at the Park were difficult, as he sought to encourage support for his plans amid a general lack of enthusiasm. There were some who did not readily accept change and several struggled to understand why horticulture should become more prominent.

Gradually, however, change came about with the help of the head of the bottom section, Dave Edgington. Working together, Tim and Dave could introduce new and exciting exhibits to the area. One of the first major projects was the renovation of the usually vacant circular reptile pit in front of the Tropical House. In addition to the aesthetics of the garden, Tim was keen to exploit the noise of birds and animals to enhance the atmosphere. Zoos had to capitalise on the unique advantage of exotic sounds reverberating among the plants.[180] For this reason, it was decided to introduce blue and gold macaws to the redundant space. An island with a surrounding moat was constructed. There were initial concerns that the macaws' housing would disrupt the visual landscape of the garden, but Tim was able to prove that planting could be used to disguise the building and integrate it into the surroundings. A pergola was built around the outside of the enclosure, with vines and kiwi fruit trained to it. The result was a simple but attractive display, with the beautiful macaws captivating visitors and giving new life to a previously overlooked area.

Carefully planned creativity

The next success came about with the necessary expansion of the meerkat enclosure in 2001. These small mammals had been kept at the Park since 1976, but the colony was now breeding far more prolifically. The first challenge faced was the provision of warm indoor quarters, as previously the animals had to be removed during the winter months to protect them from the cold. Again, there were concerns about the intrusiveness of the proposed accommodation but the macaw experience encouraged action. The innovative solution was the use of artificial rockwork to create an outcrop evoking the meerkats' native African habitat. Tim's team also took a bold gamble in developing this desert theme by planting a variety of unusual succulents and cacti in the soft earth and sand. Outdoors, the delicate specimens risked destruction by the English climate, but underground heating was installed and it was hoped that the walls would shelter the plants from cold winds. They had to be well established in protective nooks before the inquisitive animals were re-introduced, but a few plant casualties still pained the gardeners. The final modern addition was a web camera focused on the enclosure, ensuring people could enjoy the antics of the creatures in the comfort of their own home. The meerkat exhibit became a prime example of Tim's energetic attempts to encourage ambition and creativity in the partnership of horticulture and animals at the Park.

Radical alterations were also made to the general flowerbeds within the Walled Garden, as Tim sought to juxtapose formal and informal planting. The Oxfordshire attraction had officially become 'Cotswold Wildlife Park and Gardens' by 2000. More vibrant displays were thus required to justify the increased horticultural profile. Throughout the summer season, visually striking blooms in the hot colours of red, orange and yellow were abundant. *Canna* and *dahlia*, with their many distinctive varieties, were especially popular. In addition, more unusual foliage broke up the open space, with several different textures provided by *yucca* and *phormium*, large-leafed banana plants and long strands of perennial grasses such as *miscanthus.* The whole setting began to form a meandering jungle in which visitors would discover a new exhibit around each corner. Great care, however, was required to create well-defined and maintained displays. Experimentation with different varieties and colour helped discover unusual styles for maximum impact, but once a good combination was found it was reused elsewhere in subsequent seasons. Tim's ambition was partially tamed by the cautious planning of central projects, so the element of risk was constrained and he was rewarded with very few failures.[181] Despite the transformation of this space, however, Les's legacy was not forgotten. A flowerbed was maintained in his characteristic style to honour his memory.[182]

The wider grounds featured a diverse range of planting themes to appeal to the senses of visitors. The objective was to ensure their mood undulated between the relaxed tranquillity of wandering among the grounds and the stimulation created by the 'wow factor' of a vibrant horticultural exhibit.[183] In the shady woodland by Bradwell Grove station, a collection of large tree ferns, *rhododendron* and *camellia* could be found among the established evergreens. Bordering the African

Plains paddock, a lot of work was invested in 'savannah-like' ornamental grasses inter-planted with herbaceous perennials. As the scale was much greater in this open space, the style had to be far simpler but still retain a strong visual impact with depth through distance.

Back in the Walled Garden, a water garden redeveloped in 2006 displayed magnificent aquatic plants. These included the giant Amazon water lily, the only place in the country where it could be found growing outdoors. The overall result meant that, in Tim's view, there were very few British gardens which could match the diversity and integration of the Wildlife Park.

A strong team

Success also depends on a strong team and fortunately the gardening department was never found wanting. In the first few years, Les was mainly dependent on the help of two retired farm workers from the estate, George Pitelen and Sid Simpson. By 1974, Norma Martin, the wife of the new estate herdsman, heard from John Heyworth that they were struggling to cope with the work required, following the Park's rapid expansion. Despite also caring for her newborn baby, Norma started to work part-time in the gardens, helping to pick out the seedlings for the summer bedding. She really enjoyed the work and continued for 17 years, appreciating the community at the Park, as well as the extra income. Involved in every job, from planting bulbs to raking up leaves, she really felt part of the whole gardening project and proud whenever she overheard compliments from visitors. Not all people were so polite and Norma remembers a teacher and a group of schoolchildren trampling over a flowerbed she had just freshly turned over, as she looked on in astonishment.

Stressing that a great deal of hard work was expected, she also had a lot of fun working with the other gardeners. Describing it as a "family atmosphere", she said everyone got on well and looked out for each other. Inevitably there were a few cross words, usually when things were getting hectic in the spring and summer, but these were quickly laughed off and forgotten. She particularly enjoyed working with Les Scott and Bernard Castle, the under-gardener who joined the Park in 1972 and stayed until his retirement in 2003.

Alf Simpson was another popular character in the gardening department, whose "silly inane jokes" and toothy grin would have

Norma in stitches.[184] Alf had started work on the estate in 1939, when he was just 16. After a career driving tractors and trailers, taking cattle to market and horses to stud, he thought his working life was over when he reached retirement age of 65 in 1988. He was surprised, therefore, to find John Heyworth visiting him at his cottage one evening soon after, offering a position in the gardens as part of Les Scott's team. As estate staff had little contact with the Wildlife Park, this was Alf's first real experience of the place but he quickly settled into its community. Working on a part-time basis for three afternoons a week, Alf with his familiar flat cap could be found sweeping, planting and taking tea breaks with as much enthusiasm as gardeners half his age. In this way, he clocked up another two decades until his final retirement in September 2010. This made the 71 years he worked at Bradwell Grove a record unlikely to be broken in the near future. Not all the gardeners lasted for quite as long. In 1983, the Park had agreed to support a Youth Training Scheme organised by Oxfordshire County Council, combining education with practical experience. Participating in the horticulture programme, a student was to spend four days a week working as an under-gardener for Les Scott. The candidate was hopeless, however, and struggled through just three months of a year-long tenure before John Heyworth was forced to write to Cannington College, asking for an "*intelligent* keen ex-student" to replace him.[185]

It is not possible, alas, to record the experiences of everyone on the gardening staff but Norma and Alf's memories generally reflect the happy time of their colleagues. Described as "a jolly good lot", everyone was friendly and ready to have a laugh,[186] although this sometimes got them into trouble for being too chatty and overrunning on breaks. Friendliness was put to more effective use when talking to the visitors. Norma particularly enjoyed these opportunities to talk to the public, providing information and advice. One of Alf's stories displays a unique example of this public service in action, as well as showing the playful nature of the team. One day he was working by the lion enclosure with his friend George Phipps when a woman asked the two men what they would do if the big cat escaped. George explained that they certainly wouldn't be able to outrun the beast and not a lot could be done but stand their ground and throw muck in its eyes as it bore down on them. Unsatisfied with this answer, the lady asked what would happen if there wasn't any manure available. "Madam," exclaimed George, "my trousers would be full of it!" Luckily the lady shared his sense of humour and her scream of laughter could be heard on the other side of the Park.[187]

Tim Miles was quick to praise the enthusiasm and interest of the team he inherited from Les, some of whom who had already worked in the gardens department for a number of years, such as Geoff Richens, a very industrious and resourceful man, Bernard Castle and Richard Axtell, who arrived at the Park in the mid-1990s and came to be a crucial and long-serving member of the team. In 1999, Tim was lucky to gain Christine Beausire as his deputy and she played a major influence in the progress made, working closely on landscape and planting designs. When hiring staff, Tim was keen to recruit based on attitude and aptitude, not necessarily horticultural experience. This generally succeeded in maintaining a tight and stable department, made up of ten full and part-time individuals in 2010, still working just as hard as the three men who started in the Walled Garden in 1970.

For many years before Tim Miles's arrival, the apparently relaxed working ethic of the gardeners provoked much teasing from the keepers. Their shift officially began at eight but they were the subject of a running joke: "You can set your watch by the time the gardens department start work... twenty to nine." The grounds and gardens at the Park, however, have been remarkably transformed in 40 years through the toil of many dedicated, green-fingered people. The contribution of Les Scott was invaluable, enhancing a beautiful setting for the delight of millions of people. In more recent years, Tim has taken the design in a different direction, revitalising the aesthetics with enthusiasm and energy to create renewed interest. Memorable and striking exhibits carry on the Victorian tradition of striving to produce cutting-edge horticulture. Past and present, a skilled and amiable department with a fun-loving attitude helps make the Wildlife Park a success. Finally, a philosophy that always inspired Les continues to be practised after his departure: "This generation's gardeners are planning the next generation's gardens."

Chapter 10

Vital cogs

Staff behind the scenes

As expectations of zoos changed over the years, the animal keepers became more visible during opening hours and increasingly provided the public face of the Wildlife Park – but a host of other jobs needed to be performed in order for the whole venture to run smoothly. Pay-booth workers admitted the streams of visitors; office secretaries dealt with spiralling administration; shop assistants sold gifts and refreshments while a dedicated team of 'hygiene specialists' ensured a reputation for cleanliness. Success brought a rapid increase in the number of staff members and the Park became a major employer in the local area. Work for keeper family members could always be found if it was desired and residents from surrounding communities were drafted in during the busy summer season. These vital cogs made the Park machine fully functional. It is not possible to detail all their work in full, but the experiences of a few characters can shine some recognition on their colleagues and successors.

In 1970, Eileen Manley began helping to run the pay-booth at weekends and school holidays, a job she would occupy until her final retirement in 2000. Although trained as a nurse and working in Uganda during her youth, she returned to Britain and eventually earned an education degree through the Open University, proceeding to teach science at the local convent. She had originally contacted the Park to enquire about jobs for her two young boys, Gerry and Will, but unexpectedly became closely involved herself. Eileen began work the day after the Park opened for the first time, according to a 1970 rota. She earned £5 for 18 hours each weekend, selling tickets on Saturday morning and the whole of Sunday, and refreshments on Saturday afternoon. When her husband, John, also started to work there, the Park became "very much a way of life" for the whole family.[188] It required surrendering traditional activities, such as Sunday lunch and Bank Holiday outings, but they loved working at the place. Eileen enjoyed interacting with the general public, becoming friends with many season ticket holders who came to enjoy the Wildlife Park regularly. There would even be concern if familiar faces did not turn up as expected.[189]

The first pay-booth was a simple wooden hut, considered temporary as changes to the entrance drive were expected when capital became available. In the end (as with many temporary buildings at the Park), it was made to keep going for years and was not replaced until 1987, when a more solid building was built slightly further down the existing drive. John Taylor, the consulting friend from Cricket St Thomas, had advised John Heyworth not to invest in cash registers, as they were "dead money".[190] Eileen and her colleagues were therefore required to be very quick with mental arithmetic. Payment by credit card was non-existent until the Park had been established for many years, only being introduced at Easter 1987. All the money was collected in pouches, put in a small strongbox under the counter then periodically transferred to the safe in the main office. A small cash fortune, however, could be accumulated in just a few short hours before receipts were tallied and it was taken to safety. Although an alarm system was later installed, Eileen was relieved that no opportunistic thief ever took advantage of the early lack of security.

Above all else, Eileen was struck by the friendliness of the people arriving at the Park, only remembering one or two incidents of rude or uncooperative behaviour. Her favourite part of the job was meeting visitors from every part of the country, especially when using the portable ticket machines on busy days to deal with the rows of traffic.[192] On quiet days, however, the pay-booth could feel lonely and isolated. Normally, only one person would be working there and they were only relieved for a short break at lunchtime. A flask of tea or coffee was a necessity in the early years, as there was not even an electric plug socket for a kettle. In the winter, a lot of time would simply be spent listening to the radio or reading a book, interrupted only intermittently by the arrival of a visitor. With no official closing time, the pay-booth could also be open surprisingly late on dry, light evenings. However, the loneliness became rarer and the working hours more regular from the 1980s. Having experienced her workplace grow larger, more technical and safety conscious in order to modernise,[192] ill health finally forced Eileen to retire in 2000, ending 30 years of a Manley presence at the Park.

For a number of years, Eileen also supervised the team of evening litter-pickers, after her day's duties in the pay-booth were over. Once the Park was closed to the public, local youngsters, often the children of staff, would earn a small wage for collecting litter. In 1985, they received £1.05 an hour but, if they were lucky, were also allowed to keep any coins they found during their work. As young boys, Will and Gerry Manley fast realised that the adventure playground was the ideal place to discover loose change, as excited children often dropped their pocket money.

Considering the number of visitors passing through its gates, the Park was kept in immaculate condition and this encouraged further respect from the public. As a complimentary letter of 1992 noted, "a distinct lack of tasteless amusements and 'theme park' atmosphere must obviously encourage a more caring, responsible person".[193] Nevertheless, the physical expanse of the Park meant it took the litter team two hours every night to cover all the ground and everyone from managing director to trainee keepers would automatically stoop to collect any litter they spotted, determined to maintain the Park's well-earned reputation for cleanliness.

Alongside the help of the litter pickers, a small but dedicated hygiene department was responsible for the bulk of cleaning at the Park. As much as offering interesting animal exhibits, John Heyworth had recognised the importance of providing well-maintained visitor facilities from the beginning. A clean environment and tidy conveniences were crucial for general public satisfaction and encouraging return visits. A strong female cohort, made up mostly of wives of keepers or airmen from the nearby RAF base, fulfilled this duty with aplomb over the years. To illustrate the scale of their task, 7344 rolls of toilet paper and 4000 black bags were used in 2008. Since the introduction of section head meetings by Colin Fountain, they have always been represented and involved at the management level. Like many staff behind the scenes, however, they rarely received public recognition for their services. It was greatly appreciated therefore when the Park won a succession of awards for cleanliness in the late 1990s, peaking in 1999 with Loo of the Year in the Leisure category for England.[194]

The hard work and commitment of Sue Keep, the Park's long-serving hygiene manageress, was central to achieving and maintaining these high standards. Sue was raised in the small village of Langford, just four miles from the Bradwell Grove estate, and her first job was at a watch factory in Burford. Having worked at the nearby Bradwell Grove hospital in the 1970s, she already knew the Park well when she was employed as a seasonal cleaner in March 1986.[195] At that time, there was only one full-time cleaner and local women with families took part-time roles, as the hours and location were convenient. A permanent position arose for Sue and in due course she became head of the department. Due to the nature of the work, staff turnover was relatively high but Sue built a close friendship with Rita Lane, her colleague and another Park veteran. They became a formidable hygiene partnership for 19 years and, in Sue's words, "the keepers knew when we were here!".[196] It was a sad day for Sue when Rita retired with her husband, keeper Rod, in 2011.

By 2000, seasonal cleaning work was phased out in favour of four permanent full-time employees for the department, which retained expertise and provided stability. The team is responsible for all public-facing areas of the Park, such as toilets and indoor viewing areas, as well as the offices and classrooms in the Manor House. Every month, Sue and her staff also take a short trip from the Park to clean Holwell Church, of which the Heyworth family are loyal patrons. Since starting in 1986, health and safety regulations have caused an increase in paperwork for Sue, especially for risk assessments and controlling the various hazardous substances required at the Park. The day-to-day routine remains relatively unchanged, as the hygiene team's areas of responsibility have simply been refurbished rather than radically overhauled.[197] Improved technology, however, has allowed the cleaning to become more efficient and effective, and it continues to enhance public enjoyment of the Park.

Catering of good quality and value is another crucial element for the reputation of any British family attraction. Unfortunately this was a relatively weak link in the Cotswold Wildlife Park chain for many years, in spite of the best efforts of some hard-working and popular catering managers such as Keith Widdows and John Boxall. The restaurant was run as a concession from the Park's opening in 1970, meaning a contracted company provided all meals available to visitors. In 2000, it was decided to bring the restaurant under the direct control of the Heyworth family, guided by consultant Piers Sturridge. Steve Spooner was appointed as catering manager and he was charged with establishing an in-house facility that set about providing improved food and service.

Steve was raised in Norfolk and started his working life with a farming apprenticeship on the Sandringham estate. Fortunately for the Park, however, he changed career direction and gained qualifications in catering and hotel management. After working for several pubs, the London Youth conference centre in Amersham and the National Trust, Steve spotted the job advertisement for the Park in a catering magazine and decided to apply on a whim. It was only when he first arrived for his interview that he truly understood the scale of the place. He immediately recognised that there was "something magical" about the Park and he knew it was where he wanted to work.[198] Taking up his new position in October 2000, his first task was to refit the entire kitchen, servery and dining area. During the whole period of renovation, the Park never stopped serving food and used the Orangery as a temporary restaurant. Despite the scepticism of many of Steve's colleagues, the new facilities were installed and operational in time for a pre-booked dinner party just weeks later.[199]

Steve found this first season to be the hardest, faced with the dual challenge of moulding his staff into a new way of working and responding to the needs of visitors. Experience, however, made subsequent seasons easier and the transformation of the restaurant has been pivotal in the Park's recent history – the catering team works hard to exceed visitor expectations.

The shops and refreshment kiosks were also vital visitor facilities requiring an effective staff team. The original gift shop was very different from its replacement beside the Walled Garden, as it was housed in a rather bare room in the Manor House. It was run in the first year by Ann Sinfield, the curator's wife, until Keith Cousins and his family took over the responsibility. An extraordinary range of products was initially on sale, from barometers to artwork. Profits, however, were mediocre and it took several years to develop a successful business model, focusing on cheaper souvenirs and toys for children.

Sales improved when a special unit was built overlooking the car park in the mid-1970s. This incorporated a refreshment kiosk at one end, a gift shop, a garden centre and John Stone's first butterfly display. In the main shop, products were placed on a large wooden table in the centre of the room but the assistants, without cash registers, struggled to keep an eye on all their customers. Between 1983 and 1986, further improvements were made by a young and energetic woman called Isobel Teer. She transformed the shop area from being "uninspired and unimaginative"[200] into one of the key attractions at the Park. The old garden centre was replaced with a specialised children's gift shop, while her sales background was invaluable in enhancing the Park's retail operations.

Following Isobel's emigration to Australia, Joan Alderson was appointed shop manageress, overseeing its smooth running and gradual improvements over the next decade. A special section was added in March 1992, selling higher quality toys than the usual plastic creepy crawlies and pocket money gifts. A new picnic kiosk was opened between the gift shop and the children's shop in 1996. The following year, the other units were renovated, with the children's and toy shops combined into one all-embracing unit. When Joan took her well-deserved retirement in 1998, Kevin Spicer joined the Park as retail manager for the shops and kiosks. For him, "retailing is always... an opportunity to have fun,"[201] and he particularly enjoyed selecting interesting products and selling to the Park's visitors. During his first six years, another complete refit of the shop unit was required, a new store was built and the provision of refreshments was improved, helping profits increase by 300% from 1997. Kevin and his veteran team, well supplemented by students during the high season, rose to the challenge of increasing sales from a declining number of visitors, which was a general trend among British zoos.

Beginning work in the refreshment kiosk in 1975 and only retiring in 2009, Betty Vincent was the longest serving employee in this area. Living in the nearby village of Westwell, she decided a job was required to fill her time after her youngest son started going to school. Applying for a part-time position after hearing the Park was recruiting staff, she proceeded to work almost exclusively in the kiosk by the Walled Garden for the next 34 years. Like the pay-booth, working in the kiosk could swing from being unbearably hectic on busy days to lonely and boring when the Park was lacking visitors. During winters in the 1970s and 1980s, the small kiosk could become so cold that she needed to move into the gift shop to share a bit of warmth and company. As Betty's working location was so central, she would often see the bottom section keepers and gardeners, including her husband Sammy, socialising at their morning break. Despite the relatively monotonous routine, her job was made interesting by the many different people she got to meet, especially the loyal core of season ticket holders who would often recognise her. It was this enjoyment, as well as the convenience, which ensured she stayed in the position for so long.[202]

One of Betty's closest friends, Mavis Coupar, also worked at the Park, representing the final section of dedicated staff, the office team. Teased as 'Mave the Rave' by her colleagues, she first started working in the kiosk for a couple of summer seasons from 1981, before helping out in the gift shop. After a short break, she then returned to the Park to take up a job as an office assistant. She explained this meant she was a 'jack of all trades' involved in administration, working alongside key people such as Park secretary Maureen Clifford. She would often help Maureen attend tourist exhibitions and other promotional activities but a lot of time was spent on less exciting tasks, such as answering the phones and operating the switchboard, long before the advent of computers and email. Like many Park secretaries over the years, she was puzzled by the number of requests to speak to people who didn't work at the Park, such as Mr G Raff, Ali Gator or Don Key. Other duties included collecting the takings from around the Park for the office, performing First Aid when required, counting out everybody's wages and generally doing a lot of running around.[203]

Mavis has many happy memories of the Park and she described it simply as a "beautiful place to work".[204] On his retirement from the RAF, her husband Bill joined too and for many years ran the Park's train. Her colleagues were fun and entertaining, perhaps best demonstrated by a running joke about the 'knicker brigade'. Every September, the Park was very popular with female pensioners, who took the opportunity to enjoy a day trip while the weather was fine but the children had all returned to school. When taking a rest on the benches, these elderly ladies became notorious for inadvertently displaying their undergarments to the rest of the world.[205] Such moments were always guaranteed to raise laughter among the working community.

It was with great regret that Mavis had to give up her job when she moved away in 1997 but, as for all their long-serving employees, the Heyworths were very pleased to offer her life-long free admittance and welcomed her back as often as she was able. Mavis subsequently said it felt just like returning home whenever she visited, highlighting the strong affection for the Park felt by many staff, no matter their position or length of service.

Since Mavis's retirement, the office operations developed considerably as a result of technological innovation. The Park celebrated the beginning of the 21st century with a website, while a page on the social networking site Facebook was established in 2009, becoming very popular with regular visitors. Technology was also vital for improving links between wildlife collections and managing animal transfers, aided considerably by computerised, comprehensive animal records. The management of such complicated affairs required the employment of the Park's first full time registrar, former keeper Louise Peat. Just as the animal keeping staff had experienced, office roles ultimately became more defined and delineated. Considering the scale of the venture, however, the size of the administrative team remained small, especially in comparison to the bureaucratic charitable trusts running similar collections.

Every member of staff performs an important role in ensuring the Park runs smoothly and earns its reputation. Animal welfare, conservation efforts and education are all closely entwined with the success of visitor experience, which ticket admissions, catering and retail staff, office administrators and the hygiene team all enhance. Although separate from the keepers, the interviews and personal memories of just a few of these staff show that they can be no less dedicated and attached to the Park and its community.

Chapter 11

Work and play

Living at the Park

For many staff, the Wildlife Park has not been merely a workplace but a social community, with all the associated benefits and occasional disadvantages. Living on site or nearby on the estate, most keepers have been neighbours as well as colleagues. Without easy access to other social groups, the environment might sometimes prove claustrophobic, while rumour and tension could run rife. But generally there have been friendly relations among the staff, with a lot of time spent together outside work. Overall, the friendly community has helped people feel welcome and meant that many have not wanted to leave.

One of the major attractions for keepers considering a position at the Park was the inclusion of accommodation. Many cottages had been built to house the historically large estate staff and, as this group declined, they were made available for a new generation of Wildlife Park workers. The early employment process included tours of possible lodgings, so that newly hired members of staff could move into the home of their choice. Most of the desirable cottages were well-situated in the peaceful countryside, with cosy rooms and large, attractive gardens. Other properties were of variable condition, however; Simon and Diane Blackwell remembered viewing the largest house on the estate, by the old airfield, which was impressive on the outside. Upon opening the front door, however, they discovered straw and chickens tumbling down the stairs.[206]

With accommodation tied to the job, keepers could enjoy a healthy relationship with a landlord they knew well. They were able to live in beautiful, old houses which would normally be beyond their means. Many did not have to worry about mortgages until they moved jobs and required their own property. There were, however, some disadvantages. The houses were without central heating, relying on Rayburn ranges and open fires for warmth. During cold winters, frost would form on the inside of the walls.[207] For many years, the money was simply not available to make improvements but when Reggie Heyworth became more active in the Park's management, major renovations were undertaken. Also, as the number of staff increased, the population pressure required extra accommodation. Modern houses and bungalows were thus built on the old hospital site across the road from the Wildlife Park, and more were added periodically, enabling the Park to continue providing a variety of single occupancy and family houses, which were much in demand.

The gothic-style Manor House at the centre of the Park has also been used to house employees from the very beginning. In 1969, one of the first major projects was making one flat habitable for Brian Sinfield and his wife Ann, at the top of the impressive stone staircase. On the other side of the house, the first animal keeping team, all young, free and single, lived in a number of flats provided on the first floor. As a boy, Will Manley would secure a key from one of the residents to go up on the roof, which was a fantastic place to explore and sunbathe.[208] The ground floor of the manor was dark and foreboding so improvements were eventually made in this area, although the Victorian family portraits and other decorations have remained largely unchanged throughout the Park's history. The flats are presently used by several young keepers and as temporary accommodation for students on working placements at the Park.

The Manor House, however, was not necessarily ideal accommodation for some people, as it was supposedly haunted. Over the years, people reported a number of strange and mysterious spiritual experiences: the fingerprints of a child appearing every night on the glass of one room; eerie music heard out in the courtyard; a ghostly boy inhabiting a bathroom. An ethereal grey lady, suspected to be the Manor's mistress in centuries past, was seen occasionally roaming the upper rooms, while horses' hooves were often heard outside. One keeper supposedly awoke to feel his head being held down and his hair pulled back by invisible hands. For those who were sceptical and followed a more rational perspective of the world, the Manor's reputation simply offered an opportunity for fun. It was rumoured that the Manley boys once made their way into the loft above a keeper's bedroom and dripped pig's blood onto the sheets below, almost scaring the poor man to death. Simon Blackwell also enjoyed playing on his colleagues' fears. Lurking low in the dark corridor one night, he grabbed the legs of Barry Graves as he walked past, causing him to leap high in the air in shock. Simon swore he had never heard a Welshman scream so hard in his life.[209]

Young families

As demonstrated by the arrival of the Blackwells and the Lanes, there was a shift from single keepers to youthful families by the late 1970s. Rod Lane, for example, had been keen to move his children away from the crowded environs of Coventry to the safer, rural peace of Cotswold Wildlife Park. The difficulties of transport, particularly if one lacked a car, could enhance the feeling of isolation and make the life of a teenager difficult. Younger children, however, had a fantastic experience growing up in such a spectacular place. They had an adventure playground right on their doorstep and were able to roam freely around the Park, entertained by the fascinating array of animals and birds. It helped that there were several children of a similar age, such as Jeremy Bainbridge, Simon Martin, Robert Blackwell and Rachel Lane. At one time, John Heyworth had to get a bus shelter built on the road just outside the Park, so that they could all get to the local school easily.

There were also plenty of job opportunities to earn money, from litter picking to working in the restaurant or gift shops. Reflecting back, some of the parents believe the interaction with a range of people from such an early age helped develop their children's independence and confidence.[210] Now, as adults, the children only regret that they cannot offer the same experience for their families.

Many wives were kept busy as they juggled raising a family, a part-time job at the Park and socialising with their friends on the estate. For several years, Diane Blackwell worked in the shop for four hours a day, until returning home to meet the school bus, and throughout the summer holidays.[211] She appreciated the fact that the children were always welcome at the Park's organised social events, which helped make up for the pub trips she had to miss. At weekends, she felt she had dozens of readily available babysitters, who would watch over her children whenever they were around the Park. The keepers were excellent with the kids and would always let them get involved in their work to keep them entertained. The village-like atmosphere also promoted a strong social life among the wives, with afternoon teas, Tupperware parties and evenings drinking wine while the children slept upstairs. Norma Martin, another mother, described raising a family at the Park as "wonderful" and "always entertaining", with the children far luckier than their city peers who had never seen livestock or interesting wildlife.[212]

Social events

There was also a healthy range of social events for everyone to get involved in, and any excuse for a party was taken. Often hosted by John and Susan Heyworth, they provided an opportunity for estate and Park staff to mix together. Christmas was the most anticipated item in the social calendar. Christmas Day was the only time when the Park was closed to the public but keepers still had to fulfil their animal care routine. They could, however, look forward to a couple of special things at this time. Bottles of sherry, then wine in later years, were given to every member of staff by the Heyworth family. The main celebration was the infamous party, held in the old dining and drawing rooms of the Manor House and fulfilling all the expectations of a typical office party. Children had their own event, with a visit from Father Christmas, organised for years by Rita Lane. This was probably for the best, as the adults certainly knew how to let their hair down when they had the chance, judging from the photographic evidence. Traditionally, everyone turned up in fancy dress, with some impressive efforts going into the costume-making. It was an opportunity for the louder and more adventurous characters to shine, with cross-dressing and extensive use of make-up often featuring. Supported by music, food and free drink, it was a social highlight for many.

Each summer, John and Susan Heyworth held a garden party at their home. Everyone with a close connection to the Bradwell Grove estate was invited, from Park keepers and office workers to the woodsmen and gamekeepers. It was a chance for people who normally missed out on social events to mingle and meet others. The boots and waterproofs had to be swapped for more formal attire and the archive photographs show some rather dubious fashion trends down the decades. Former staff have fond memories of the occasion, which frequently seemed to be blessed with good weather. They enjoyed delicious food and the wine was poured generously by John Heyworth. The evening was consequently very lively, and fully clothed dips in the outdoor swimming pool were common. The invasion of the garden one year by neighbouring cattle, however, was less predictable. Eventually the number of staff grew so large that gatherings at the Heyworths' home were no longer possible and the Park itself became the venue for such events. Barbecues and clay pigeon shoots have since replaced the garden parties as the social occasions of the summer.

Some of the most amusing memories concern the donkey derbies run at the Park in the 1970s and 1980s. They had initially begun as an additional public attraction for charity, with the first organised in 1974 in aid of the Injured Jockeys Fund. Ken Bedford, who managed the pony rides during the high season, also offered the use of his animals to staff on fine summer evenings. They would then organise races, either being drawn in a trap or, more painfully, riding the donkeys bareback. Will Manley recalled spending an afternoon building small wooden jumps to add an even greater challenge to the course. The indignity of being carried off into the distance with no control of one's mount was suffered by many. The donkeys had no respect for the working hierarchy and the keepers enjoyed this social levelling, although the atmosphere could get very competitive. One year, curator Bob Golding lost the first race so strode over to the winner, reptile keeper Glyn Evans. "I'm your boss, give me that donkey," he demanded, and subsequently won the next race.[213] Rod Lane remembers once dodging guy-ropes and canvas as his lively beast careered through the tents and caravans of a campsite at the bottom of the field. He said that one could always spot the experienced riders, as they would remove all the keys and objects from their pockets, to avoid any accidents when the inevitable fall came.[214] As everyone got involved and was prepared to look silly, the donkey derbies were great fun enjoyed by all.

A competitive streak among Park staff, however, was never far from the surface and would appear during the many organised sports events and competitions. Teams made up of the top and bottom sections gave the opportunity to extend the friendly working rivalry into the social scene. Winning in football, volleyball and rounders matches was taken very seriously. Sometimes the Park would put these differences aside and come together to face an outside team. In the late 1970s, Park and estate staff competed for the Bradwell Grove Rugby Challenge Pot, although the Park held the advantage by recruiting some talented public school boys to play. Following the main match, a game against the women was played, in which Barry Graves broke his ribs but still ended up at the pub afterwards. Inter-zoo competitions between keepers also became more common, with sports matches and quizzes helping to facilitate contact between British collections. The tradition currently continues, with spontaneous events occurring throughout the summer. Rugby, however, has been replaced with five-a-side football, with recent success in the Oxford football league.

The most anticipated moment of any Park sporting event was, arguably, the trip to the pub afterwards. The frequent pub trips were as integral to the community as tea breaks and family life. Despite the relative isolation of the Wildlife Park, there were several drinking establishments available to the staff. In the early years, the keepers received their cash wages in little brown envelopes on a Thursday every fortnight. They would then head into Burford for the evening to celebrate with a few pints. Sometimes the young and single men were drawn to Swindon, the nearest town with any nightlife. A job as an animal keeper was generally good at attracting female interest but one of the first keepers had a unique and innovative tactic for guaranteeing attention. This involved smuggling a tame leopard cub out of the Park and into the club. A lot of the time, staff would take the far simpler option of going to the bar at Bradwell Grove Hospital on the other side of the road, until the hospital closed in 1985. The Park also had its own bar installed when a liquor license was granted in 1975. This was open to the public for daytime drinking until the late 1990s but would be brought into action for staff from time to time. Whatever the personal pub preferences over the years, conversation would typically gravitate to work and animals.

Finally, members of staff have always been involved in charitable fundraising events. Most early efforts focused on pet shows and festivals, supporting charities of particular interest to John Heyworth. There was once a wishing well garden between the restaurant at the rear of the Manor House and the original puma enclosure. This earned thousands of pounds for the Cancer Research Campaign, with which the Park had a long-standing association. It disappeared in 1993, however, when the restaurant toilets were built. Charitable efforts were consequently directed more towards conservation and the breeding of endangered species. Strangely, most enthusiasm was shown if an event included dressing up and being ridiculed. Perhaps the best illustration of this commitment was demonstrated by the World Wildlife Fund 'Running Wild' event in November 1986. Celebrating 25 years of the WWF, people all over the country had 12 hours to travel as far as possible from their local zoo. Ten teams departed from Cotswold Wildlife Park, including keepers Simon Blackwell, Terry Hornsey and Nigel Platt. Dressed as a lion, a bear and a gorilla, they were able to travel to Miami with sponsored flights from Virgin Airlines.[215] National fundraising days have continued to be well supported with big donations and funny costumes, raising the Park's profile while making a significant contribution in a fun manner.

There is a danger of presenting the Park as a utopian society, where community was everything. Of course, that could not be the case. Like any other workplace, tension, bitterness and rivalry among colleagues were encountered on occasion. The tranquillity of the Oxfordshire countryside could become confining, particularly if personal transportation options were limited. Older workers were more distant from their younger peers and less inclined to get involved, particularly if it meant breaking into a keepers' clique. The stories, however, show that there was a remarkable ability to push any grievances aside and work professionally together, which was an absolute necessity in such a small community. Moreover, the advantages far outweighed any rare disagreements. As former staff looked back to past decades, the unanimous message was of a close, friendly community which formed a strong affectionate bond. In more recent times, the population has become more diverse and disparate, but inclusive social events are still popular, widely promoted and crucial to general happiness. Essentially, the Cotswold Wildlife Park has always been more than merely a place of employment. It is a family whose members, in the words of Lillian Scott, work and play hard, enjoying life.[216]

Chapter 12

Family charm

CHILDREN AT THE PARK

Cotswold Wildlife Park was created by John Heyworth with the intention of preserving the Manor House and grounds for the purposes of public recreation. Despite all the conservation and education concerns of modern zoos, they can only be successful in these areas if they also maintain a reputation for an enjoyable and affordable day out. Although the Park appealed to many different types of people, families clearly made up the majority of visitors. During the summer months, the grounds were packed with thousands of primary school children. When term started again, the excitable crowds retreated to be replaced by groups of adults strolling around with little ones who were too young for school. Over the years, millions of bouncing children have dragged their long-suffering parents all over the Park, desperate to see the rhinos, the vultures, the snakes and the other animals which caught their imagination. Fortunately, three additional attractions have helped offer brief moments of peace for the adults in an extremely busy day, because others took over the role of entertaining their offspring. As a result, they have enjoyed the adventure playground, pony rides and the miniature railway as much as the kids.

First, no self-respecting family attraction could survive without an adventure playground. It started off from humble beginnings. In 1969, John Heyworth had made several enquiries to the makers of quality children's play equipment. The expenditure was simply too high, especially considering his other priorities and rapidly accumulating construction costs. When the Park opened, therefore, there were only swings and a seesaw available, built by the estate handymen. Crucially, however, they were in a prime location, between some woodland and the large picnic lawn at the rear of the Manor House. The trees were perfect for climbing and exploring, while the neighbouring grassy space was an open play area. During fine weather in the summer, this would be packed with people eating, resting and watching their children. Mothers could relax because they thought the whole environment was safe, public and visible.[217]

For the first few years, new apparatus was added to the playground frequently, but it was all built by Park staff using readily available materials. In the winter of 1970, a log climbing frame was constructed from timber felled on the estate and climbing nets were suspended from the trees. A simple mound of earth was added to the landscape, intersected by a large culvert pipe through which children could crawl. In the spring of 1973, a fort was built on an enormous upturned tree stump, while a playhouse in the shape of an animal was added, although the intended species was not easily identifiable. This was a time with little red tape or safety regulation, before rubber matting came to replace sand or bark chippings on the floor. As long as common sense was employed and the equipment was solid, additions were simply dictated by what it was thought children would enjoy. Famed for his thrift, John Heyworth wrote to the local fire service in January 1984, seeking help in acquiring a decommissioned fire engine for the playground. One was eventually found and brought to the Park. The most iconic and long-lasting feature of the playground, however, has been the tree house and slide, first installed in May 1977. During a great storm, an ancient Cedar of Lebanon had been dangerously damaged. The trunk was left standing about 20 feet high and a long, steep chute was installed. Since then, seeing brave children climbing the steps with trepidation then flying down the slide laughing has been one of Susan Heyworth's favourite things about the Park.[218] A few moments watching the sheer delight on their faces could reflect the pure enjoyment of the whole day out.

For many years, just beyond the adventure playground was a small paddock surrounded by a rustic fence. In 1969, Ken Bedford, living locally in Burford, had heard excited talk about a wildlife park being established down the road. Foreseeing a profitable opportunity, he contacted John Heyworth and offered to provide donkey rides for visitors on busy days. Starting with a Shetland pony and five donkeys, one loaned to Pets' Corner, the attraction quickly became a cheap and extremely popular money-maker. At the beginning of the summer season, Ken would roll up with his animals in a trailer, ready to put the paddock to good use for a few months. Then, as the nights started to draw in, he would disappear for another year. In 1970, it cost 9 pence for a donkey ride and 1 shilling for a pony ride. Small carriages, or traps, were also available for a little extra.

Helping with the rides was a useful part-time job for the friends and family of many Park staff, including Rod Lane's wife, Rita, and Norma Martin. In fact, this early work experience helped start a life-long passion for horses in the daughter of kiosk worker Betty Vincent.[219] The days could be long and hard, and Norma remembers that they could rarely take a break, because the queue was always too long.[220] A continual stream of children needed to be helped onto their ride, using a small log mounting stump, before being led in a circle around the paddock. Each trip was only short, occasioning some grumbles from more thrifty parents, but miles could be walked each day by the helpers. The last rides were given in April 1991, as a result of Ken's retirement, and the space was absorbed into the Children's Farmyard.

Miniature railway

Trips on the miniature railway were a highlight for people of all ages from 1974 on. Initial objections by the council, however, meant that the clickety-clack of the train and the toot of its engine might never have been heard. Upon first seeing the proposals in October 1973, certain council members raised serious concerns. They felt that it would introduce an "unnecessary commercial element virtually unconnected with the use of the Park" and would be the "first step in destroying [the Park's] existing character".[221] They had to be taken to see an existing railway at Warwick Castle in order to prove the appropriateness of the venture and dispel their doubts. They insisted that the passenger-carrying railway be used primarily as a practical means of transporting visitors around the Park, rather than as a recreational attraction. Over the years, fortunately, this attitude has changed.

After reaching an agreement with John Heyworth and finally securing the approval of the council, the owner, Keith Fenwick, installed and operated a small length of two foot gauge track for the 1974 season. During the winter, this limited service was extended by nearly a mile and the new layout was officially opened on 27 April 1975. The original hope was for a Blue Peter presenter (John Noakes, Peter Purves or Lesley Judd) to do the honours but, in the end, the duty fell to Desmond Morris, naturalist and regular ribbon-cutter at the Park. The track was not a complete circuit but ran from Bradwell Grove Station, by the owl aviaries, to Panda Terminus near the front of the Manor House. Two diesel engines, painted red with a glossy black funnel, ran in opposite directions, each pulling two beige passenger carriages with capacity for up to 50 people. By 1976, Wallaby Junction, next to the lake, allowed the trains to pass each other and another station, Leopard Halt, was built close to the big cat enclosure. Instead of one standard fare, it was calculated according to the station stops.

Despite its appeal to visitors, the railway did not always run smoothly and there was an occasionally fraught relationship between Park management and the concessionaire. On 20 October 1976, John Coborn wrote to Fenwick, complaining of the weeds, debris and general rough environment around the track, which was his responsibility to maintain. Furthermore, he was concerned that "the carriages are never secured and [when] unattended, children delight in pushing them up and down the track". With a lack of safety awareness, it was fortunate that no accidents occurred. The partnership continued for a while longer but, at the end of 1981, the Park purchased the railway and took all responsibility for its operation.

The following year, the stations at Wallaby Junction and Leopard Halt were closed. Trains now simply ran between Bradwell Grove Station and Panda Terminus, renamed Tortoise Terminus after the giant tortoises replaced capybaras in the neighbouring enclosure.

Shortly after the takeover by the Park, the need for a more professional running of the railway was urgently brought home by a worrying incident on 11 August 1982. Mischievous children had jammed open the points of a crossing and then moved the point indicator so the driver could not spot the problem in time. The train derailed and one of the carriages was toppled on its side, leaving its passengers shaken. Fortunately they were only dazed and not seriously injured but, uncertain of appropriate procedure, they were allowed to drift away without follow-up checks. Hearing of the accident, the railway inspectorate later arrived, demanding the immediate closure and complete overhaul of the track in preparation for the 1983 season.

From this point, the attention to safety standards was radically improved. Steve Scarrot, one of the Park's handymen, was appointed the first railway supervisor, a role occupied by a member of the maintenance team ever since. Weekly inspections were made mandatory, together with detailed records of all repair work and incidents. A close working relationship was also forged with Alan Keef of Ross-on-Wye, who was a light railway engineer. His skills and expertise were vital in keeping the track, engines and carriages in the best working order.

A third engine, dark green with a bright red buffer plate, was brought into service at the beginning of the 1990s. It was frequently driven by Bill Coupar, the husband of Mavis who worked in the Park's offices. Having been in the RAF all his life, Bill was persuaded to drive the train one busy weekend when there was a desperate shortage of staff. He enjoyed running it so much that he became a permanent fixture of the team until his retirement in 1996.

The current engine, the fourth and similar in aesthetics to its predecessor, was ordered in October 2002, to be ready for the next Spring Bank Holiday weekend. The diesel hydraulic locomotive has a gross weight of 4 tonnes and cost £51,200. Named Bella to commemorate one of the original white rhinos which had recently passed away, it has since pulled thousands of visitors around the Park. Finally, the railway circuit was completed five years later, with Tortoise Terminus removed and additional track installed to link to Bradwell Grove Station. Opened on 5 May 2007 by the Park's local MP David Cameron, train passengers could now enjoy a full tour around the Park, invariably eliciting smiles and waves as they passed by. Even the moodiest teenager or coolest university student could regress to simple childhood when riding the Cotswold Wildlife Park miniature railway.

The 'Junior Friends'

'Tracks' of a different sort were also associated with another area of entertainment for children. This was in fact the name of the newsletter for the "Junior Friends" of Cotswold Wildlife Park, a club for young visitors and nature enthusiasts. It had been started in January 1982 by Peaches Golding, the wife of the curator, but after she left, Maria Fountain decided it was a worthwhile scheme and took the project on.[222] Originally inheriting just eight members, the group had grown to over 400 by 2000. For a small annual membership fee, they received a free admission ticket, a Park poster, a badge and four copies of the 'Tracks' newsletter. Maria recollected that child visitors to the Park would excitedly identify fellow members, proudly wearing the round badge with its distinctive paw print on an orange background. In the days before the internet and social networking websites, contact among the 'Junior Friends' was surprisingly global. It was realised that links could be built with the many visitors from abroad and, in March 1987, 'Tracks' announced plans for an international pen pal scheme. From that point, many children sent in descriptions of their personal interests, their contact details and a request for letters. The people involved were as widespread as South Africa, India, America and Australia.

The newsletter was the crucial pillar for this youth group and it was the most regular Park publication until the main *Wild Talk* newspaper was revived in 1993. Recent stories about the Wildlife Park, particularly new arrivals, were eagerly anticipated by its young readers. The articles about endangered wildlife and Park animals were accessible and informative. Jokes, puzzles and quizzes completed the content, which Maria thought was a "lot of fun" to create. Its production, however, was a long process which had to be started at least a month before its release. A clunking typewriter was needed to write each article, before a master copy was compiled with pictures, scissors, glue and a lot of patience. Hours would then be spent at the temperamental photocopier, with the inevitable jamming and misprints causing no end of frustration. Once the newsletter was put in order and stapled, the addresses were all handwritten and the envelopes individually stamped. The bumper Christmas issue doubled this workload. Maria found her reward with the many letters from inspired readers, although the 'Junior

Friends' were very adept at pointing out any spelling errors.

The charm of the Wildlife Park for many parents has simply been its strong family-friendly atmosphere. Even when the place was busy, it never seemed crowded and there was little danger of a child being lost. If young minds ever drifted from the appeal of live animals, they could soon be entertained by pony rides, train rides and the adventure playground. The Heyworth family and the Park staff have long realised the importance of such a reputation. Like the council members who feared the installation of the railway, they have always been keen to avoid the commercialisation of the grounds. Although ticket prices had to rise to cover expenses, efforts were made to keep a day out at the Park affordable and without hidden costs. It is for these reasons that many people who grew up visiting the Park returned with their own little ones to pass the pleasures on to the next generation. The overwhelmingly positive reaction of children and their families to the Park has made the whole venture hugely worthwhile for John Heyworth, who has taken great satisfaction in seeing his own childhood home put to good use. He said the public enjoyment of the Park made him feel "absolutely delighted".[223]

Chapter 13

"Learn something about animals and birds"

Education at the Park

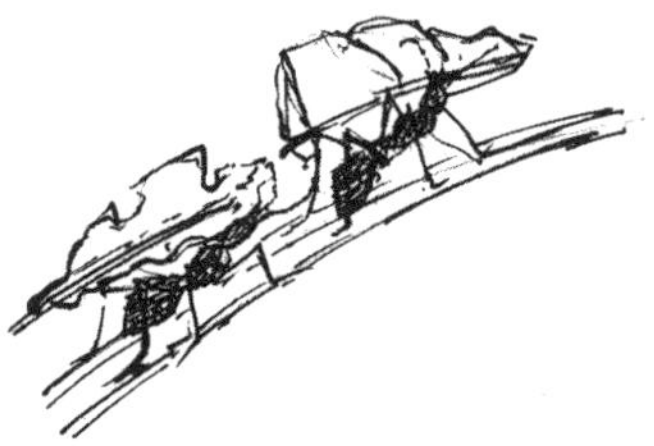

Writing in December 1969, John Heyworth told the biologist Peter Scott that he hoped his new enterprise would "put the house and gardens to good use by encouraging townspeople to come here and learn something about animals and birds".[224]

Growing up on a country estate had given him the opportunity to learn about the natural world in a manner which evaded many other people. For many years, the city zoos, with their cramped conditions and concrete cages, had been the only outlet for curiosity about wildlife. Such menageries remained predominantly concerned with entertainment. Those days, however, were passing and the Cotswold Wildlife Park was among a new generation of attractions that integrated teaching with recreation. Ever since the gates were opened to the public, therefore, education was a central pillar of the Park's life and work. As always, plans were limited by available funds, meaning ambitious schemes were sometimes not practical. Progress, nevertheless, was gradually made; as zoos increasingly came to justify their existence through their educational role, the ability to engage effectively with schools and the wider public became a priority for all members of the industry. The Park had to become more organised and efficient in fulfilling this obligation, but the original goal remained the same.

Michael Molesworth was the crucial figure in this area of the Park's early history. A retired Oxford educator, he spent a number of years running a field studies centre with his wife Rosemary in Alvescot, a picturesque village just two miles from the Park. Children from across the country would take part in their week-long residential courses, with organised educational day trips to local Cotswold attractions. Upon hearing about the forthcoming wildlife park at the end of 1969, he made contact to see if a working association could be fruitful. After some negotiation, the Park's first educational department came into existence. The arrangement was stronger and more comprehensive than Michael had originally envisioned. Two rooms in the Manor House were put at his disposal, becoming a lecture-room and a working classroom. He and his wife were responsible for cleaning, equipping and maintaining these spaces. The Park then became the centre of a wide-ranging science course, with biology lessons, animal observations and studies. Groups of 28 children, accompanied by three teaching staff, would arrive at the Wildlife Park on their first day for an introductory talk and tour. They would then begin work on their allocated projects before returning by minibus to the residential accommodation in the evening. The routine on subsequent days was packed with lectures and projects, interspersed with sandwiches for lunch, breaks on the adventure playground and lemonade and buns as an afternoon treat. For schools too far away to make an independent day visit, these longer courses proved extremely popular.

There was no guarantee of such an enthusiastic response. Indeed, in the initial contract negotiations, Michael insisted a variety of possibilities were considered, "ranging from howling success to abject failure".[225] Fortunately, the partnership between Park and educator proved to be a happy one from the beginning. John Heyworth was particularly satisfied with the financial return of the contract. At a fee of £1 per child per week, to cover the entrance and use of facilities, Michael Molesworth was bringing in a steady income. In return, Heyworth only needed to provide some otherwise unused rooms and the services of a keeper for eight sessions a week, who would give tours, talks and information. Lacking the necessary experience in his existing complement of staff, Mr Heyworth was content to let the education department be run fairly independently, especially as he personally liked Michael and was confident in his abilities. The teacher enjoyed collaboration with the Park staff, was not possessive of his enterprise and would willingly take suggestions on board. In retrospect, Mr Heyworth felt that he owed him a great deal for his dedicated work in founding an official educational role at the Park and forging connections with schools.[226]

Plans for an Education Centre

In less than two years, the success of the department encouraged the two men to think more ambitiously, focusing on educational aspirations beyond simple financial benefits. It had quickly become clear that the existing facilities were inadequate to cope with demand and, in order to expand, a dedicated building was required. Architect Michael Drew was thus commissioned to design an Education Centre to be erected at the Park. This was to be situated behind the adventure playground and next to what became the tradesmen's entrance. The intention was to provide one of the best facilities of its kind in the country. A large, tiered lecture hall was considered essential, surrounded by study rooms and practical areas. A library and even a museum space were included in the original plan. Provision for closed circuit television, tape recorders and cameras was also required, as the Park was apparently "being used as a testing ground for audio-visual aid equipment". A dark room would allow students to develop their own photographs, while a projection theatre could show nature films and documentaries. Hot food from a canteen would ensure packed lunches were to be a thing of the past. Moreover, a large aviary, full of native flora and fauna, or a vast aquarium was to be installed by the entrance, as a focus for observational studies. The whole unit, finally, was to be made accessible for physically handicapped students, which was a very progressive consideration for the time.

In order to realise this vision, Cotswold Wildlife Park Educational Committee was formed at the end of 1971 and registered as a non-profit charitable organisation. Michael Molesworth, John Heyworth and Brian Sinfield were all members of its governing body, along with a number of local notables with interest or expertise. This included the director of education for Oxfordshire County Council, Mr E J Dorrell. This suggests an attempt to build links with local government, although the relationship failed to produce any financial grants to help the scheme. The involvement of Commander

Henderson, from the British Council for the Rehabilitation of the Disabled, demonstrates the commitment to addressing access issues in their plans. After the initial meetings and discussions, an appeal was launched to raise the vast sum of £250,000 required to fund the proposal. Leaflets were produced and widely distributed, displaying a plan of the potential centre and outlining its objectives. The overriding duty of the committee, it declared, was to help "educate children in natural history subjects and to make them fully aware of the problems of worldwide conservation".[227]

Within a few months, however, grave concerns were being raised about the scale of the initiative. An emergency meeting of the committee was called in July 1972. After half a year, expenses of £2641 had accumulated, covering the architect's fee, Michael Molesworth's salary and the printing of the appeal leaflets. The only income had been a £2000 donation from the Park and a paltry £24 from public donations, leaving the accounts dangerously in the red. Committee members were told that the proposed sum was considered unattainable by a professional fundraising organisation, which had advised John Heyworth to make it a dormant company. After a long and frank discussion, they decided to persevere for a while longer, reducing the target budget to £50,000. This could fund a simpler building, one full-time salary and maintenance costs. MPs were lobbied, local authority grants were sought and personal contacts at the World Wildlife Fund were tested but still no significant progress was made. The young Park simply lacked the experience or reputation to gain high-profile support. At the beginning of 1973, John Heyworth once more wrote to the committee, highlighting the "serious doubts as to the feasibility of [their] rather ambitious plans".[228] By the end of the year, his colleagues all agreed and the scheme was placed into 'cold storage' until a more opportune time, which had yet to emerge four decades later.

Despite this disappointment, and the obvious limitations of its facilities, the education department continued to thrive. In 1975, under a new ten-year agreement, the three rooms above the Reptile House were leased to Michael Molesworth, in addition to the lecture room in the Manor House. He was to do all the alterations and decoration needed to prepare them as education areas, while the Park was responsible for installing heating, electricity and all major structural repairs. With this additional space, a modest expansion of educational efforts was possible, without the need for an expensive new building. Aimed mainly at children aged between eight and twelve, the lessons sought to encourage thinking about animals, their environment and the importance of conservation. Topics included 'Vanishing wild animals', 'Mathematical aspects of the Park' and comparisons of predators and their prey.

In 1978, the brass rubbing centre in the former dining-room of the Manor House was added to the department's responsibilities. This had been established two years earlier, in conjunction with the World Wildlife Fund. The charity had provided large brass plates featuring endangered wildlife, information leaflets and school worksheets. Using paper and wax materials to create the print, apparently "the result of some ten minutes' concentration and enjoyment is a souvenir which could last many years".[229] Rent was waived by John Heyworth in return for re-decoration of the room, and the Molesworth education enterprise grew once again.

School parties

Throughout the first decade, therefore, the Park was mainly reliant on the Alvescot Field Studies Centre, with its residential courses and local education authority contacts. When Michael and Rosemary Molesworth sadly separated in 1979, their involvement in education at the Park also ended, leaving it directionless for a time. Day visits by schools in the local area had been run since 1970 and obviously these continued. A special rate was available for large school parties, with one accompanying adult gaining free admission for every 20 children. As long as members of staff were available, keeper talks and guided tours were given at no additional charge. Study pamphlets and worksheets suitable for a range of ages were offered at a small fee. Frequently, however, school trips were simply an end-of-term treat for the children, a jolly outing rather than an outdoor activity linking to a project back in the classroom.[230] Despite living right on its doorstep, keeper Simon Blackwell's children enjoyed their school fun trips to the Wildlife Park because they could show off how much they knew about the place to their friends. The only problem arose when they had to return on the coach and get the school bus right back.[231]

Partly from experiences with his own children, Simon Blackwell saw the need for the Park to develop an educational emphasis in its own right. If a visit could be made more relevant by linking it to an ongoing school project, the demand for day trips would be greater and learning about zoo purposes would be reinforced. Together with Maria Fountain, they built contacts with relevant people at Oxfordshire County Council, seeking advice and support. By 1984, local teachers were taking secondment opportunities to work at the Park. Undergoing a temporary placement, with their own teaching post covered, they would use their expertise to liaise with schools and organise educational facilities. During such a scheme, a particularly good relationship was built with a respected local teacher called Bill Ashbridge.

In the summer of 1986, Bill became the external adviser to the recently established education unit, which was the first such formal organisation by Park keepers. After confirming Simon and Maria as education officers, the first meeting explored the main areas where improvement was required. They identified a need to reach out to neighbouring counties, to take advantage of the Park's prime location. It was also concluded that the dated worksheets needed revising. It was essential, furthermore, that the educational aspect of the job was made more appealing to other keepers. The "open nature of the work of the unit" was broadly advertised, along with "the assumption that all staff are partners in the venture to the extent that they wish to be involved".[232] Everyone was invited to contribute to new information leaflets by submitting notes on their special interests. Most importantly, these interests could also form the basis for lectures by the keepers themselves.

The reptile keepers were the first to work with school groups regularly, as they had more manageable creatures which could be presented and touched. In the summer, head reptile keeper Don Reid could expect to give at least one talk a day, usually many more.[233] With no set framework or lesson plan, he could talk at will about any animal or subject he had chosen for that occasion. Generally, these were received with excitement and enthusiasm by the children, even if some of the more herpetophobic teachers were unwilling to participate. He remembered showing some young yellow rat snakes to a group of children in one of the rooms above the Reptile House. They all queued up willingly to be bitten by their tiny fangs, very excited by the harmless, tickling sensation. After every meeting with a school group, Don would like to give naturally inquisitive children the opportunity to ask questions. Sometimes, however, he had to give up on a lost cause: concluding a talk on snakes one day, Don was met with a wall of blank faces and a long silence, until one hand at the back was slowly raised into the air. "Excuse me," enquired the boy, "Is there a bin somewhere for my crisp packet?"

Talks by animal keeping staff were not a particularly new innovation, but they had been infrequent. At the beginning of the Park's history, Brian Sinfield had been a guest at many local clubs and societies, frequently taking an animal to contribute to his presentation. They were very advantageous in encouraging word of mouth knowledge of the Park, particularly by branches of the Women's Institute. The opportunity to meet staff had also been a highlight of Michael Molesworth's residential courses. Only a relatively small number of keepers, however, had the confidence or will to speak publicly in the early years. Maria Fountain had been reluctant until she was coaxed into a talk by curator Bob Golding. She was surprised to find that she enjoyed the interaction with people. She came to recognise that the people who worked with the animals every day could give the most informative talks with a more natural flow. Often the passion of the speaker would shine through and connect with the audience.[234] From the safety of mucking out enclosures behind closed doors, the keepers were increasingly brought to the stage to inform and entertain. In order to overcome remaining hesitancy, a monetary incentive was introduced by the education unit, with a fee for each talk paid to the keeper and a commission collected for special educational projects. At the same time, the Federation of Zoological Gardens was promoting greater engagement with visitors as a sign of a responsible zoo committed to its wider obligations. In fact, education was a key aspect for consideration during the inspections introduced by the Zoo Licensing Act of 1981.

More than simply lecturing people, however, it was important to make a lasting impression. Whereas the first school residential courses had been mainly concerned with observational study, there was a shift to more engaging techniques as education was delivered to the wider public. "Saturday Workshops" for children first began in the winter of 1986, when keepers had more time available. Children would spend two hours with Maria exploring a topic such as 'Colour and camouflage' or 'Venomous animals'. After a short talk, they would feel teeth, claws and other objects, meet some animals of the Park and discuss their findings before concluding with a fun quiz. Simon Blackwell recalls giving regular visitors a metaphorical "smack on the back of the head", meaning a memorable experience which remained with the listener when they had returned home.[235] Close contact with an animal was the perfect method. Snake handling days at the Park were first officially advertised in 1985 but had been run on an informal basis for much longer. Eric, the beautiful tame python, was a regular attraction with Don Reid. Reptiles, however, were not to everyone's taste and other alternatives were explored. "Animal Encounters" were first begun in 1997, with opportunities to gain hands-on experience with the residents of the Children's Farmyard, including the Shetland ponies, rabbits and ferrets. The scheme was extended over the following years and visitors could now book meetings with more exotic creatures such as the tapirs, capybaras and lemurs.

Exhibit signs

A far more subtle and widespread teaching method, however, was the signage visible at each animal exhibit. Throughout the Park's history, these signs have been frequently reviewed and have evolved significantly. In March 1970, a visiting friend of John Heyworth's could only make one criticism: the "insufficient descriptive labels" which meant people did not know what the animals were.[236] Acting to remedy this, the early plaques included a painting of the creature on display, with its common and Latin name and its country of origin. Over time, photographs replaced the paintings, although they were not universal even in 2001, when some visitors were left frustrated that they could not identify the animal they were observing.[237] Information was also added, often written by the keepers. John Stone almost had an entire scholarly paper next to his leaf-cutting ant exhibit, describing the intricate workings of the colony. While this could be extremely interesting to a few visitors, the majority of zoo-goers would walk on after a couple of minutes. Obviously a balance had to be struck for maximum impact despite a limited attention span. Efforts to chronicle the natural history of a species were abandoned in favour of one or two short, interesting comments. Always aware that it must balance teaching with recreation, the Park's prevailing philosophy hoped that visitors would leave remembering a couple of these facts after an enjoyable day out, so signs were left concise.

The value of the Park's education policy was always linked to the degree of collaboration with local schools. By the 1990s, teacher secondments were no longer possible and the department was entirely the responsibility of keeping staff. In 1992, after a few years of falling school visits, Simon Blackwell decided to involve practising education professionals in a rethink of strategy. Poor attendance at an open day for teachers in October was disappointing, demonstrating some limitations in the Park's contacts. However, the meeting produced full and frank discussion. The report pleasingly noted a real enthusiasm for development and willingness to take part among the keepers. Teachers were still struggling with the new National Curriculum, introduced by legislation in 1988. Although the curriculum meant a revision of all worksheets, leaflets and talks, it offered an opportunity for zoos to integrate their efforts more closely with schools. By the end of the 1990s, eight keepers were regularly giving talks and acting as a "great educational resource on important subjects such as conservation and animal behaviour". Feedback from teachers was also continually raising standards.[238]

After Simon's departure in 1998, Nathan Crockford, a senior keeper in the Walled Garden, became particularly involved in the education committee. He took up the role championing a greater degree of public interaction by staff. He recognised that the animal presentations were still "fairly low-key" but was optimistic that, with time and confidence, they would further improve. One example of the progress made was provided by the parrot talks, introduced by a young keeper named Darren Fellowes in 2003. He trained a pair of scarlet macaws to fly right over his audience's heads, a blue and gold macaw would perch on his hand throughout and two yellow-thighed caiques were tame enough to be handled by the public. Given daily throughout the summer, talks supposedly 15 minutes long could end up three times that length. Another example was the introduction of a talk by keepers to accompany penguin feeding time, always a popular fixture in the day. This allowed keepers to get across a conservation message while the penguins bobbed and dived for the sprats thrown into their pool. These, and the popular birds of prey flying demonstrations run by Geoff Dalton of the Cotswold Falconry Centre over summer weekends and Bank Holidays, were the perfect proof of the value of such presentations for inquisitive audiences, passionate keepers and iconic animals.

A new education co-ordinator

In May 2004, the decision was taken to professionalise the education department further and Joyce Farquhar was employed as the Park's first dedicated education co-ordinator. A key aspect of her role was helping the keepers make the most of their presentations. She offered advice on public speaking and how to deal with small children. She also had to liaise with schools and teachers, arranging individual requirements and adapting every visit to suit the work back in the classroom. With risk assessment forms and other rising bureaucratic obstacles, educational school trips had declined since their peak in the late 1980s. A co-ordinator was vital in facilitating the organisation of the visits and encouraging their continuation. Joyce and her successor Bob Joiner, another former teacher, helped ensure school education at the Park was enjoyable, relevant and worthwhile for children from a wide range of backgrounds. As she explained, however, the animal husbandry staff remained at the core and there was "nothing like the look on a child's face when confronted by a real live zoo keeper, fresh from tending the animals".[239]

Education, therefore, has always had a strong presence at the Park but it has progressed a long way since the first residential courses led by Michael Molesworth. Although the early and over-ambitious plans of a teaching centre never materialised, the whole Wildlife Park could be used as a unique outdoor classroom, as recognised by the Park being the first zoo to receive recognition (in the form of a quality badge awarded in 2009) from the Government's Council for Learning Outside the Classroom. Lessons became more interactive, the topics were more encompassing and Park policy was tied closer to the needs of schools and the curriculum. Most important, however, was the increasing engagement of keepers with the wider public, fulfilling one of the crucial obligations of a modern, responsible zoo by spreading their interest and passion.

The intimate involvement of the keepers has always been a

defining characteristic of Cotswold Wildlife Park's educational output which distinguishes the Park from other major UK zoos: for the most part, those have teaching staff in education departments largely distinct from those at the sharp end of animal husbandry. This difference is what continues to make the Park's approach so unique and rewarding for keepers and pupils alike.

The enthusiasm of the keepers was infectious, particularly for younger visitors who would return home inspired to write letters and draw pictures. These demonstrations of enjoyment were rewarding for all involved, although sometimes the Park could not win every battle for young hearts and minds. After an informative day meeting the animals, ten-year-old Stacey Funnell wrote, "I didn't like the way the dead chicks were put into the owl's cages. I do understand that they have to eat, but I think owls should be vegetarians." Learning, like development of the Park's educational policy, was a gradual process.

Chapter 14

"The best wildlife park that no one has ever heard of"

PUBLIC RELATIONS & PROMOTION

"How many people are coming through our gates?" This was the one all-important question forever concerning the Park's management. With no outside funding from the EU, the government or the local authority, income from visitors is entirely responsible for keeping the animals in the best possible conditions, maintaining the Manor House and grounds, and allowing progressive improvement. Park promotion, therefore, has been vital for attracting new customers and reminding previous visitors to call again.

At the beginning, interest had to be generated by whatever means possible, before a reputation was built and word of mouth could kick in as the cheapest form of advertising. Personal recommendations are limited in their scope, however, and money had to be invested in marketing to keep the profile up. The Park's public relations machine has involved a surprising number of people over the years, from celebrities to animal keepers and office secretaries. It became increasingly more sophisticated, which was the result of experience but also necessity, as competitors and the types of media outlets increased. Considering the British attraction to anything with fur or feathers, virtually any story about animals could secure coverage, but the challenge was always to maximise impact.

The first curator, Brian Sinfield, was mindful of the importance of receiving good press. At the time, zoos could be fairly ruthless in the exploitation of their animals. Brian knew one collection which would happily parade a delicate baby elephant along the main street of a town on a cold winter's day, as long as they secured a photograph and article in the next day's paper.[240] Brian was not averse to attracting attention in a similar manner, as long as it was not harmful to the animal's welfare. In autumn 1973, a leopard cub had been born after some complications. The subsequent necessary medical care ensured it grew close to its keepers. At 11 weeks old, the cub was taken to a local Burford pub to meet the married owners, who had cared for orphaned leopards in India. Christened 'Jan' with a sprinkling of best bitter, the local newspaper editors could barely contain their excitement over the cute, fluffy bundle. The next year, Jan did not appear so sweet and innocent during her television debut on *Blue Peter.* She spent most of her appearance straining to get at the throat of an older leopard, which was busy chewing on its handler's glove.[241]

Brian found, however, that it was the unplanned occurrences which would seize the imagination of the media. In spring 1972, four rockhopper penguins had been introduced to their Humboldt cousins in the pool of the Walled Garden. Exploring their new enclosure, they proceeded to jump up the rocky landscape which formed the central waterfall, before lining up along the artificial cave. One bold bird then leapt another three feet to the top of the garden wall, before hopping onto the adjoining roof of the refreshment kiosk and plunging another nine feet down to the ground to make his escape. The first two times 'Houdini' achieved this feat, he was recaptured on nearby paths in the Park, but the third occasion he was discovered by a motorist two miles away. A film crew from regional television was contacted and the whole episode shamelessly staged, including the roadside capture of the runaway. This time, however, he was "popped into our van conveniently blazoned with the Cotswold Wildlife Park crest".[242] Re-enacted for yet another media company the next day, the film was sold and shown on the national *Nine O'Clock News.* Houdini never made his way back to the Antarctic but, after earning his new home valuable publicity, he settled well into his now escape-proof enclosure.

The Park guidebooks

Brian was also responsible for the Park's first guidebook, always an attractive souvenir for visitors as well as a modest way of boosting income from the gate. He described the first edition as a "rather rushed affair", and difficult to illustrate, as there were no Park animals to photograph at the time.[243] Instead he toured other collections and snapped pictures of species he intended to display. A transparency of a pair of Canada geese, taken years previously and cropped to remove excess scenery, was used as the coloured front. Unknowing visitors later remarked that this was an excellent cover shot. Despite the problems encountered, the guidebook was quickly prepared and printed, with an initial run of 45,000 copies costing £1000. Over the next decade, the publication improved with each edition, with more pages and vibrant colour photographs, this time actually taken at the Park.

Between 1970 and 2010, there were 15 different guidebooks, acting as a valuable chronicle of the Park's development. In the research for this book, the centrefold maps were a useful indicator of changes and additions to the animal exhibits. Pictures of Park scenes, mostly attributed to Colin Fountain, who combined being curator with being an accomplished photographer, also offered particularly interesting visual evidence. Their intended use for visitors, however, was to offer information on the different areas of the Park and highlight species of particular interest. The text was full of interesting facts to supplement the educational signs around the Park. In 1992, a local artist was commissioned to draw a set of black and white images of certain animal features, such as hoofed feet and a bat's wing. Since then, these have been used in every edition. From 2000, there have been some more notable additions, as the Park itself underwent more radical development. More attention was paid to the gardens, in order to raise their profile as a significant aspect of the attraction. Additional pages were required to include new exhibits, such as the Madagascar walkthrough. The overall result has been a comprehensive and glossy account of both the Park's steady evolution and essential continuity.

Witnessing most of this progress, there was one key person at the heart of the Park's advertising and promotional material for over 30 years. Maureen Clifford, friendly and approachable, originally took up a secretarial position in October 1978. Arriving for her interview, she remembered being told to drive straight up to the Manor House, where she was warmly greeted by John Heyworth, who promptly told her to drive back to the main car park.[244] Despite this first impression, the meeting went very well and Maureen began work in the main office with John Coborn and John Vickers. Her time was mainly spent answering the phone, typing up letters and dealing with the petty cash, which kept her extremely busy. Previous secretaries had only held the position temporarily, moving on after a couple of years. In his letter offering the job, John Heyworth wrote, "I do hope you will be happy with us and will be occupying that centre room for a long time."[245] His judge of character proved exceptional once again but at that point even he could not have expected the length or scope of Maureen's career at the Park.

When reflecting on her time at the Park, Maureen was at a bit of a loss to describe how she came to be responsible for advertising. With very little experience of public relations before arriving at the Park, the role seemed to creep up on her. Between 1981 and 1983, Peaches Golding had been particularly influential in organising newspaper reports and similar media opportunities. As a secretary, therefore, Maureen was involved in the arrangements and received guidance from the Goldings. Following their departure, and with more staff covering secretarial duties, she gradually came to devote more time to the Park's promotion while still being involved in the bustling office. Most attention had to be paid to communications with magazines and local newspapers, identifying the relevant publications and ensuring the right messages were being put across. In terms of selling points, Maureen believed the Park was unique in its beautiful natural setting and was clearly a family venue, but which also remained appealing to people of all ages.[246] A yearly routine emerged, with fairly standard seasonal press releases. Every spring, the newspapers would include a feature on the latest notable births, particularly if any young animal was cute and being hand-reared. In summer, the press would be informed about the details of special weekend events and how popular the Park was proving to be. In winter, news would focus on how the animals coped with the cold weather, with rhinos ploughing through the snow, or how keepers worked on Christmas Day. In these months, Maureen's advertising focus would shift to indoor attractions, such as the warm Tropical House.

Trade fairs

Among Maureen Clifford's earliest responsibilities was the running of advertising stands at trade fairs around the country. Showcasing days out at leisure attractions, these special exhibitions were either open to the general public or invited delegates from organised tour companies. John Coborn had been particularly interested in taking part in these and had enlisted Maureen's help in the late 1970s. They would take along a number of display boards decorated with posters and photographs. She would then spend the whole day handing out leaflets and chatting with people. In this manner, they could help organise trips and build links with coach companies and similar organisations. Maureen particularly enjoyed meeting the general public and personally selling the Park, especially when children showed a strong interest. Mavis Coupar, another long-serving stalwart of the office, remembered having "lots of fun and a good laugh" travelling with her and helping out at these events.[247] Throughout the 1980s and into the early 1990s, this was a very popular and worthwhile method of promoting the Park, as they were attended by thousands of people. This has declined more recently, however, with the wider accessibility of information on the internet.

At Maureen's first such event on her own in February 1979, she succeeded in generating publicity from an unexpected angle. At this time, tame animals were frequently taken to accompany the Wildlife Park's stall, which made the display stand out. On this occasion, Maureen had taken a cockatoo from Pets' Corner to an exhibition at the Brunel Centre in Swindon. Early in the morning, as she turned back from a group of women, she noticed the bird had escaped from the cage and was calmly sitting by the opening. Approaching softly, Maureen attempted to coax the cockatoo back into the cage. It stubbornly refused to surrender its newfound freedom, perching on a spectator's head before flying off into the beams at the top of the centre. It proceeded to spend the whole day flapping around the roof and 'sabotaging' other displays with its droppings. Returning to the Park, Maureen was convinced that she was going to be fired for losing the bird, but John Coborn was simply delighted that the story had made the *Swindon Advertiser*. Simon Blackwell managed to catch the escapee later that evening and its keeper cleared Maureen of any error after admitting that she had been given the wrong cage.[248]

The tourist boards were the main organiser of these exhibitions, but they also provided important advice and contacts for Maureen's work. The Park had first joined the Thames and Chilterns Tourist Board in 1977, following a need to increase publicity after disappointing visitor numbers could not be blamed solely on the poor weather. The advantages were immediate, with inclusion in regular regional directories that advertised local attractions. They also improved transport links with the capital by helping to establish a weekend bus service from London Victoria to Burford and the Wildlife Park, which regularly brought summer season visitors throughout the 1980s. A long and fruitful partnership developed with Stuart Harrison, a member of the Board, who would liaise with Maureen and the management to develop effective publicity strategies. Membership of the Thames and Chilterns Tourist Board was ideal, as the Park sat very comfortably within the boundaries of that area, but the group folded in 1992. Since then, the Park has been absorbed into the much wider, and less well-defined, South East region, being advertised alongside attractions as far away as Kent.

Television coverage

While the Tourist Boards were particularly useful at facilitating radio and television advertisements, the Park had several unique tricks to guarantee free local publicity. Without a doubt, the best example of ingenuity and media shrewdness used the large snakes. During Don Reid's time in the Reptile House, an ITV camera crew from Birmingham would turn up every year to film the keepers measuring the giant anaconda. Although the snake could be carried by just two men, four or five were always used to make the feat look more impressive. Taken either to the courtyard of the Manor House or the picnic lawn in front of the restaurant, the creature would be laid out on the ground. The camera would then pan along its body as a tape measure was pressed against it by the keepers and, for many years, a remarkably high growth rate was recorded. In reality, the anaconda remained about 15 feet while the tape was deceptively bunched under the keepers' hands to distort the result. The task, however, was not without its dangers. Although usually docile, one year the animal became very agitated, suddenly struggled and bit Don hard. To his annoyance, the news clip that evening appeared to show him walking off dejectedly with a bleeding arm, rather than his subsequent 'heroic' capture of the released snake.[249] Over years of creating effective publicity and widespread interest, Park staff learned that the camera can sometimes lie.

Aside from some animals fleetingly attracting media attention, the Park has also had more permanent television celebrities in residence. In the late 1970s, John Coborn and John Stone were regulars on *TISWAS*, the Saturday morning children's television show hosted by Chris Tarrant and others. They would drive to the Birmingham television studio to show and talk about their reptiles and insects in the 'Creature Feature'. In 1979, Rocky, the captive-bred, hand-reared rockhopper penguin, and Cocky the citron-crested cockatoo, also had their big break. They became stars of BBC's *Animal Magic*, a hugely popular wildlife entertainment show, featuring Johnny Morris. Each week, the presenter, dressed as a zookeeper, would meet different animals in the studio and speak to them. Rocky and Cocky, anthropomorphised with voices from Johnny, would help him 'comment' on the featured guests. Many years later, in 1998, Mole the hand-reared meerkat became a star of the silver screen with the aid of Rolf Harris, when the *Animal Hospital Roadshow* was filmed at the Park. More recently, however, the regular keepers have become the focus of the TV cameras. The six-part documentary *Park Life* was filmed in 2007 and broadcast on ITV West the following year. Exploring the hard work behind the scenes, the programme sought to offer some insight into the friendly community and ethos driving the Park.

Many human celebrities, moreover, have been fans of the Park and happily made appearances at special events. Johnny Morris would often judge and award prizes at pet shows held at the Park in the 1970s. The entertainer Rod Hull was also a popular guest, posing for photographs with tame real emus alongside his famous but more boisterous puppet emu. Despite a broken ankle, in 1976 Jimmy Savile 'fixed it' for 150 children of staff from Broadmoor Hospital to visit the Park, where they enjoyed a ride on the new train and had a close encounter with a badger. A long standing association was established with the local poet Pam Ayres, who first found fame on the television talent show, *Opportunity Knocks.* An early poem, 'The Embarrassing Experience with a Parrot', was inspired by a visit to the Cotswold Wildlife Park and provides a perfect example of her comic verse and down-to-earth style. Her appearances at the Park included opening the Children's Farmyard in 1985 and, at the 25th anniversary celebrations, awarding first prize in the fancy dress competition to a child dressed as a cowpat.[250] In more recent times, the impressionist Rory Bremner and the comedienne Ruby Wax have appeared at the Park, supporting its events and charitable causes.

The reputation of the Wildlife Park has always been strong, but public relations and promotional work by Maureen Clifford and others was required to enhance it, spreading the word to a wider audience. The money spent on advertising steadily increased over the years, from around £19,000 in 1983 to £89,000 in 1991 and £145,000 in 2001. With a much broader scope for publicity, however, these resources had to be carefully allocated. Magazines, official guides, trade publications, newspapers, leaflet printing and distribution, promotional videos and tourist board membership all ate into the budget. Recently, the internet and other technology have forced irreversible changes in advertising, offering a multitude of alternatives. Nevertheless, there is still a place for older methods. Maureen Clifford praised magazine advertising because, despite having less immediate impact than a TV advert or newspaper article, it lingers. Copies are found in public waiting rooms two years later and, as people flick through, they are reminded of the Park.[251] The intention is to keep its name in front of the public and subtly create awareness; grand promotional stunts or constantly bragging about this year's expensive new exhibit are not considered the right style. Instead the philosophy remains to highlight the advantages of "the best wildlife park that no one has ever heard of", which is held in great affection by regulars and always gives a pleasant surprise for first-time visitors.

Conclusion

It was an ambitious gamble in 1970 by John Heyworth to open the Cotswold Wildlife Park, as he desperately tried to save the beloved Manor House on his family estate from the inexorable decline that had seen countless English country houses reduced to ruins over the previous two decades. There was great potential in the beautiful grounds but it was only unlocked with the right team. The vision was inspired by John's passion for animals, but the professional knowledge of Brian Sinfield, alongside the gardening skill of Les Scott, helped to realise it. In the early 1970s, the three men worked with limited resources but relentless energy to establish the enterprise, supported by an eclectic and youthful staff. Despite many challenges and pitfalls, the Park gradually expanded, adding new exhibits and acres. It evolved organically, with John and his employees thinking innovatively but constantly aware of what was a natural fit. As a result, its reputation also increased, becoming a firm favourite with people across the country as the word spread, and always beloved by its crucial local audience in Oxfordshire and Gloucestershire.

From the 1980s, the Park responded well to higher professional standards and growing expectations among the public. The animals had always been kept in excellent conditions but, as keepers' knowledge was enhanced by the developing communication between zoos, constant improvements were made in husbandry. Co-ordination between zoos also helped achieve more successful captive breeding programmes for endangered species, while greater efforts were made in educating the public about the animals on display and their conditions in the wild. The Park was therefore making a significant contribution when it reached the height of its popularity in 1990. Although it was affected by the steady decline of visitor numbers occurring across the zoo industry in the subsequent decade, it fared better than most and continues to attract well over 300,000 people a year. It remains a successful and well-respected member of the international zoo community, but persists in forging its own path in the 21st century rather than following in the shadow of others.

Throughout this time, the Park has stood consistently by its founding principles and maintained the ethos that makes it so popular. There is genuine attraction for people of all ages, with children fascinated by the animals and older visitors appreciating the integration of the exhibits with beautiful surroundings. The dedication of the keepers to the welfare of their animals is obvious, as is the care and attention taken to creating and maintaining natural, spacious enclosures. Despite being a private, family-owned business, which needs to make a profit to survive and prosper, the uncommercial atmosphere has always been a crucial aspect of the Park's appeal. The Heyworths were always keen to avoid investing in any expensive, transient crazes, ensuring a timeless and personal experience for all. They have often monitored visitor reactions at the entrance gate, keeping in touch with public opinion about the good value of ticket prices. Essentially, the clean, green and relaxing environment provides an enjoyable and affordable day out for everybody from young families to pensioners.

Even the most passionate visitor, however, could not match the affection for the Park held by the staff who have worked there. They have enjoyed the opportunities available in their jobs and everybody has felt part of the overall project. Involvement in such a reputable company helped several employees secure senior positions in other animal collections across the world. For many, it was also far more than a workplace, particularly in the early decades. Keepers and their families lived on site or nearby, creating a close community where wives enjoyed social evenings and children went to school together. Pub visits, sport friendlies and parties brought the whole extended family together, mixing many diverse characters. Time spent working at the Park therefore fostered many long-lasting friendships and happy memories, which have formed the backbone of this history. After retiring or moving on to other positions, many people stayed in touch and the Park retained a special place in their hearts.

It would all have been very different without the extraordinary vision and efforts of one man, the modest and gentlemanly John Heyworth. He has been ultimately responsible for the happiness of millions of visitors and hundreds of employees over 40 years. It is therefore fitting to conclude with his personal reflections on his achievement. He certainly did not expect the scale of success when he first started out and, despite the hard work, was surprised when it all "just happened".[252] He was perhaps most proud of the expansion of his staff, from small beginnings to over 100 employees.[253] Looking back on the progress of the Park, he was adamant that he would not have done things differently, seeming very happy with its natural growth and future development. Most importantly, however, he considered himself very lucky and said simply, "I've had a wonderful life... I've enjoyed it all."[254] Cotswold Wildlife Park is his beautiful legacy and it will hopefully continue to delight visitors and create fascinating memories for many more years to come.

Notes

[1] English Heritage, National Monuments Record.
[2] N. G. James (ed. A. S. Till), *Recollections of Bradwell Grove, Holwell and Burford*, 1907-1987, p 3.
[3] *Ibid.*, p 8.
[4] *Ibid.*, pp 11-12.
[5] *Ibid.*, p 12.
[6] Interview with Susan Heyworth, 2 August 2010.
[7] John Tinker, 'Bingo at the Zoo' in *New Scientist*, 9 April 1970.
[8] *Ibid.*
[9] Molly Badham, *Chimps with Everything* (London, 1979), Ch 5-11.
[10] Jimmy Chipperfield, *My Wild Life* (London, 1975), Ch 10.
[11] Interview with John Heyworth, 2 August 2010.
[12] John Knowles OBE, *My Marwellous Life: In Zoos and Conservation* (Brighton, 2009).
[13] Interview with John Knowles OBE, 30 July 2010.
[14] *Ibid.*
[15] John Heyworth Papers - File II.
[16] Brian Sinfield Papers - Letter 2, 10 April 1969.
[17] L. B. Powell, 'Where town and country meet', in *Farm and Country*, October 1968.
[18] John Heyworth Papers - File I.
[19] Letter from John Taylor to John Heyworth, 8 April 1969, John Heyworth Papers - File I.
[20] Brian Sinfield Memoirs, Ch 1, p 3.
[21] Letter from John Heyworth to John Taylor, 21 April 1969, John Heyworth Papers - File 1.
[22] Interview with Brian Sinfield, 16 July 2010.
[23] Interview with Lillian Scott, 27 July 2010.
[24] Interview with Susan Heyworth, 2 August 2010.
[25] John Heyworth Papers - File II.
[26] D. Edgington, *Cotswold Wildlife Park and Gardens: The First 35 Years of the Animal Collection*, p 24.
[27] Interview with Lillian Scott, 27 July 2010.
[28] Interview with Eileen Manley, 26 July 2010.
[29] Brian Sinfield Memoirs, Ch 3, p 1.
[30] Interview with John Heyworth, 2 August 2010.
[31] Brian Sinfield Memoirs, Ch 3, p 2.
[32] Interview with Brian Sinfield, 16 July 2010.
[33] Interview with John Heyworth, 22 July 2010.
[34] John Heyworth Papers - File I.
[35] Brian Sinfield Memoirs, Ch 7.
[36] *Ibid.*, Ch 13.
[37] Interview with Brian Sinfield, 16 July 2010.
[38] Brian Sinfield Memoirs, Ch 3; Interview with Brian Sinfield, 16 July 2010.
[39] Brian Sinfield Memoirs, Ch 3, p 8.
[40] Interview with John Heyworth, 22 July 2010.
[41] Interview with Susan Heyworth, 2 August 2010.
[42] Cotswold Wildlife Park guidebook, 1970, p 4.
[43] *Wild Life Park News*, Spring 1971.
[44] Brian Sinfield Memoirs, Ch 3, p 5.
[45] Note from Les Scott, John Heyworth Papers - File VI.
[46] John Heyworth Papers - File VII; this area was housing purple-faced langurs and lar gibbons in 2011.
[47] Brian Sinfield memoirs, Ch 4, pp 2-4.
[48] Interview with John Knowles OBE, 30 July 2010.
[49] John Heyworth Papers - File X.
[50] Inspection Report by the Federation of Zoological Gardens in Great Britain and Ireland, December 1970, John Heyworth Papers - File X.
[51] Interview with Brian Sinfield, 16 July 2010.
[52] Interview with Don Reid, 26 August 2010.
[53] See Chapter 4.
[54] Brian Sinfield Memoirs, Ch 11.
[55] *Wild Life Park News*, Winter 1971, p 12.
[56] *Ibid.*, Spring 1974, p 12.

[57] Interview with Brian Sinfield, 16 July 2010.
[58] More details about the experiences of Gerry and Will Manley at the Park can be found in Chapter 8.
[59] For more on the keepers, see Chapter 8.
[60] Memorandum from K. V. Cousins, John Heyworth Papers - File XXI.
[61] Handwritten note entitled 'Rates', John Heyworth Papers - File XXI.
[62] Interview with Brian Sinfield, 16 July 2010.
[63] Interview with Will Manley, 24 August 2010.
[64] John Heyworth Papers - File XXX.
[65] Interview with Brian Sinfield, 16 July 2010.
[66] Interview with Will Manley, 24 August 2010.
[67] John Heyworth Papers - Files XXII and XXIV.
[68] Interview with Colin and Maria Fountain, 6 August 2010.
[69] Interview with Don Reid, 26 August 2010.
[70] Interview with Will Manley, 24 August 2010.
[71] *Wild Life Park News*, Spring 1974.
[72] Interview with Barry Graves, 16 August 2010.
[73] John Heyworth Papers - File XXX.
[74] Interview with John Knowles OBE, 20 July 2010.
[75] John Heyworth Papers - File XXXIV.
[76] Interview with Colin and Maria Fountain, 6 August 2010.
[77] Interview with Simon and Diane Blackwell, 6 August 2010.
[78] John Heyworth Papers - File XLIII.
[79] Interview with Rod Lane, 24 August 2010.
[80] Interview with Simon and Diane Blackwell, 6 August 2010.
[81] Interview with Barry Graves, 16 August 2010.
[82] Interview with John Heyworth, 22 July 2010.
[83] Interview with Don Reid, 26 August 2010.
[84] *Ibid.*
[85] Interview with Colin and Maria Fountain, 6 August 2010.
[86] Interview with Simon and Diane Blackwell, 6 August 2010.
[87] Interview with Colin and Maria Fountain, 6 August 2010.
[88] Interview with Simon and Diane Blackwell, 6 August 2010.
[89] Interview with Colin and Maria Fountain, 6 August 2010.
[90] John Heyworth Papers - File XLIV.
[91] Interview with John Knowles OBE, 30 July 2010.
[92] Interview with Simon and Diane Blackwell, 6 August 2010.
[93] John Heyworth Papers - File XLIV.
[94] Interview with Will Manley, 24 August 2010.
[95] Interview with Colin and Maria Fountain, 6 August 2010.
[96] *Ibid.*
[97] Interview with Mavis Coupar, 27 July 2010.
[98] Interview with Will Manley, 24 August 2010.
[99] Michael Stourton, 'Country Notes: A farmer who went wild', *Financial Times*, 14 April 1990.
[100] John Heyworth Papers - File LII.
[101] Interview with Colin and Maria Fountain, 6 August 2010.
[102] Interview with Simon and Diane Blackwell, 6 August 2010.
[103] For more on Simon Blackwell's experiences, see Chapter 8.
[104] John Heyworth Papers - File LIX.
[105] *Wild Life Park News*, March 1988.
[106] Interview with John Stone, 20 July 2010.
[107] *Ibid.*
[108] Interview with Colin and Maria Fountain, 6 August 2010.
[109] *Ibid.*
[110] *Talk on the Wild Side*, Issue 3 (1995), p 3.
[111] Interview with Rod Lane, 24 August 2010.
[112] *Ibid.*
[113] *Wild Talk*, 2011, p 8.
[114] Interview with Susan Heyworth, 2 August 2010.
[115] Interview with Reggie Heyworth, 25 February 2011.
[116] For more information on Tim Miles's background and work, see Chapter 9.
[117] *Wild Talk*, 2003, p 1.
[118] For more information on these projects, see Chapter 9.
[119] Interview with Reggie Heyworth, 25 February 2011.
[120] I am indebted to Louise Peat for her article on the refurbishment of the Tropical House in 2004.
[121] Interview with John Stone, 20 July 2011.
[122] *Wild Talk*, 2007, p 2.
[123] Interview with Jamie Craig, 25 February 2011.

[124] Interview with Reggie Heyworth, 25 February 2011.
[125] Interview with Tim Miles, 26 August 2010.
[126] *Wild Talk*, 2008, pp 2-3.
[127] Interview with Jamie Craig, 25 February 2011.
[128] Interview with Reggie Heyworth, 25 February 2011.
[129] Interview with Jamie Craig, 25 February 2011.
[130] *Ibid.*
[131] *Ibid.*
[132] See Chapter 13; *Wild Talk*, 2003, p 3.
[133] Interview with Jamie Craig, 25 February 2011.
[134] *Wild Talk*, 2009, p 3.
[135] *Ibid.*, 2010, p 1.
[136] Interview with Reggie Heyworth, 25 February 2011.
[137] Interview with Jamie Craig, 25 February 2011.
[138] Interview with Eileen Manley, 26 July 2010.
[139] Interview with Mavis Coupar, 27 July 2010.
[140] Interview with Will Manley, 24 August 2010.
[141] Interview with Brian Sinfield, 16 July 2010.
[142] Brian Sinfield Memoirs, 'A Zoo Needs Builders', pp 6-7.
[143] Interview with Will Manley, 24 August 2010.
[144] *Ibid.*
[145] John Heyworth Papers - File XLVI.
[146] Interview with Barry Graves, 16 August 2010.
[147] *Ibid.*
[148] *Ibid.*
[149] *Ibid.*
[150] John Heyworth Papers - File XXIX.
[151] Interview with Rod Lane, 24 August 2010.
[152] *Ibid.*
[153] John Heyworth Papers - File XLII.
[154] Interview with Colin and Maria Fountain, 6 August 2010.
[155] See Chapter 13.
[156] Interview with Barry Graves, 16 August 2010.
[157] Interview with Simon and Diane Blackwell, 6 August 2010.
[158] *Ibid.*
[159] Interview with Colin and Maria Fountain, 6 August 2010.
[160] Interview with Barry Graves, 16 August 2010.
[161] Interview with Simon and Diane Blackwell, 6 August 2010.
[162] Interview with Rod Lane, 24 August 2010.
[163] Matthew Zaremba, 'Being a new keeper', *Wild Talk*, 2003, p 8.
[164] *Witney Gazette*, 12 January 1978.
[165] Interview with John Heyworth, 2 August 2010.
[166] Interview with Mavis Coupar, 27 July 2010.
[167] Interview with Eileen Manley, 26 July 2010.
[168] John Heyworth Papers - File II.
[169] John Heyworth Papers - File XXXII.
[170] Interview with Lillian Scott, 27 July 2010.
[171] Interview with John Stone, 20 July 2010.
[172] *Ibid.*
[173] *Cotswold Wildlife Park Society Bulletin*, Winter 1980/81.
[174] *Ibid.*
[175] Interview with Rod Lane, 24 August 2010.
[176] Interview with Susan Heyworth, 2 August 2010.
[177] Interview with Rod Lane, 24 August 2010.
[178] Words written by Peter Scott, Les's son, for his father's funeral.
[179] Interview with Tim Miles, 26 August 2010.
[180] *Ibid.*
[181] *Ibid.*
[182] Interview with Susan Heyworth, 2 August 2010.
[183] Interview with Tim Miles, 26 August 2010.
[184] Interview with Norma Martin, 28 July 2010.
[185] John Heyworth Papers - File XLI.
[186] Interview with Alf Simpson, 13 August 2010.
[187] *Ibid.*
[188] Interview with Eileen Manley, 26 July 2010.
[189] *Ibid.*
[190] John Heyworth Papers - File III.
[191] Interview with Eileen Manley, 26 July 2010.
[192] *Ibid.*
[193] Letter from D. Clifton, 6 April 1992 - John Heyworth Papers - File LVIII.
[194] *Wild Talk* 2001, p 6.
[195] Interview with Sue Keep, 5 November 2011
[196] *Ibid.*
[197] *Ibid.*
[198] Interview with Steve Spooner, 5 November 2011.

[199] *Ibid.*
[200] John Heyworth Papers - File XLVII.
[201] *Wild Talk*, 2004, p 3.
[202] Interview with Betty Vincent, 11 August 2010.
[203] Interview with Mavis Coupar, 27 July 2010.
[204] *Ibid.*
[205] *Ibid.*
[206] Interview with Simon and Diane Blackwell, 6 August 2010.
[207] *Ibid.*
[208] Interview with Will Manley, 24 August 2010.
[209] Interview with Simon and Diane Blackwell, 6 August 2010.
[210] *Ibid.*
[211] *Ibid.*
[212] Interview with Norma Martin, 28 July 2010.
[213] Interview with Simon and Diane Blackwell, 6 August 2010.
[214] Interview with Rod Lane, 24 August 2010.
[215] John Heyworth Papers - File XLVII.
[216] Interview with Lillian Scott, 27 July 2010.
[217] Interview with Norma Martin, 28 July 2010.
[218] Interview with Susan Heyworth, 2 August 2010.
[219] Interview with Betty Vincent, 11 August 2010.
[220] Interview with Norma Martin, 28 July 2010.
[221] John Heyworth Papers - File XX.
[222] Interview with Colin and Maria Fountain, 6 August 2010.
[223] Interview with John Heyworth, 2 August 2010.
[224] John Heyworth Papers - File V.
[225] *Ibid.* - File VI.
[226] Interview with John Heyworth, 23 July 2010.
[227] John Heyworth Papers - File XIV.
[228] *Ibid.* - File XVIII.
[229] Cotswold Wildlife Park guidebook, 1979, p31.
[230] Interview with Simon and Diane Blackwell, 6 August 2010.
[231] *Ibid.*
[232] John Heyworth Papers - File XLVII.
[233] Interview with Don Reid, 26 August 2010.
[234] Interview with Colin and Maria Fountain, 6 August 2010.
[235] Interview with Simon and Diane Blackwell, 6 August 2010.
[236] John Heyworth Papers - File VI.
[237] *Wild Talk*, 2002, p 2.
[238] *Wild Talk*, 1997, p 7.
[239] *Wild Talk*, 2005, p 5.
[240] Brian Sinfield Memoirs - 'Telling the People', p 1.
[241] *Wildlife Park News*, Autumn/Winter 1973 and Spring 1974.
[242] Brian Sinfield Memoirs, 'Telling the People', p 12.
[243] Brian Sinfield Memoirs, 'A Zoo Needs Builders', p 9.
[244] Interview with Maureen Clifford, 4 August 2010.
[245] Letter from John Heyworth to Maureen Clifford, 2 October 1978, John Heyworth Papers - File XXXI.
[246] Interview with Maureen Clifford, 4 August 2010.
[247] Interview with Mavis Coupar, 27 July 2010.
[248] Interview with Maureen Clifford, 4 August 2010.
[249] Interview with Don Reid, 26 August 2010.
[250] Interview with Maureen Clifford, 4 August 2010.
[251] *Ibid.*
[252] Interview with John Heyworth, 23 July 2010.
[253] Interview with John Heyworth, 22 July 2010.
[254] Interview with John Heyworth, 2 August 2010.

Index
of names, places and organisations

Adamson, Joy 61
Alderson, Joan 132
All Creatures Great and Small 56
Alvescot Field Studies Centre 155
Amis, Mark 66
Animal Encounters 95, 158
Animal Hospital Roadshow 169
Animal Magic 56, 169
Ashbridge, Bill 156
ASRA 45, 57
Associated Pleasure Parks 4
Association of British Wild Animal Keepers 45
Atkinson, William 1
Attenborough, David 49, 53
Axtell, Richard 126
Ayres, Pam 65, 169

Badham, Molly 4, 46, 57
Bainbridge, Jeremy 137
Bath, Marquis of 5
BBC 85, 121, 169
Beausire, Christine 126
Bedford, Duke of 62
Bedford, Ken 65, 139, 144
Bedfordshire 5, 6
Bellevue Zoo 35
Benfield, Pete 98
Birdland 86, 108
Blackpool Zoo 93
Blackwell, Diane 135, 137, 138
Blackwell, Robert 137
Blackwell, Simon 70, 107, 109, 110, 112, 135, 137, 141, 155, 158, 159, 167
Blue Peter 146, 164
Born Free 61
Bourton-on-the-Water 51, 86, 108
Boxall, John 131
Bradwell Grove 1, 3, 6, 10-12, 17, 28, 35, 41, 67, 74, 88, 98, 115, 123, 125, 130, 139, 140, 146, 147
Bradwell Grove Hospital 3, 130, 140
Bradwell Grove Station 123, 146, 147
Bremner, Rory 170
Brett, Beverly 60
Bristol Zoo 58
Broadmoor Hospital 169
Brooks, Alfred 17
Brunel Centre 167
Burford 1, 3, 12, 13, 15, 24, 65, 69, 119, 130, 140, 145, 164, 168
Burkitt, Gerald Gale 14

Cameron, David 97, 98, 147
Cannington College 121, 125
Castle, Bernard 124, 126
Catskill Game Farm 6
Charity Commission 49
Chedworth Brass Band 76

Chessington Zoo 58
Chester Zoo 35
Chilterns Tourist Board 168
Chipperfield, Jimmy 5-6, 9, 18, 28
Clifford, Maureen 133, 165, 167, 170
Coborn, John 37, 38, 44, 45, 49, 50, 56, 60, 106, 116, 146, 166, 167, 169
Cornbury Park 13
Cotswold Falconry Centre 160
Cotswold Herpetological Symposium 45
Cotswold Wildlife Park Educational Committee 153
Cotswold Wildlife Park Society 49
Cotswold Wildlife Trust 49
Coupar, Bill 147
Coupar, Mavis 99, 116, 133, 167
Cousins, Keith 43, 47, 131
Coventry Zoo 37
Craig, Jamie 90, 92, 93, 95, 97, 98
Cricket St Thomas 10-12, 85, 128
Crockford, Nathan 159
Curry, Sheila 37

Dalton, Geoff 76, 160
Davis, Stanley W 15
Davison, Peter 56
Derby, Earl of 97
Diana, Princess of Wales 75
Dix, Matthew 91
Doctor Who 56
Dorrell, Mr E J 153
Downman, Mike 70, 75
Drew, Michael 153
Drusillas Zoo Park 108
Dublin Zoo 27
Dudley Zoo 4, 56, 57, 104

Edgington, Dave 70, 86, 91, 92, 98, 112, 122
Edinburgh Zoo 44
Edmonds, Les 60
Eley, Daisy Louisa 118
English Heritage 67
European Herpetological Symposium 45
Evans, Glyn 60, 70, 74, 139
Evans, Nathalie 4

Faherty, B G 15
Farquhar, Joyce 160
Federation of Zoological Gardens of Great Britain 5, 27, 28, 46, 60, 63, 157
Fellowes, Darren 159
Fenwick, Keith 146
Financial Times 68
Fisher, Lady 72
Flamingo Park 12
Fletcher, Frank 91
Fountain, Colin 61-63, 66, 67, 76, 78, 80, 83, 85, 86, 103, 107, 109, 110, 112, 130, 165
Fountain, Maria 66, 76, 107, 110, 148, 156, 157
Fox, Samuel 2
Fox, William Henry 2
Frankfurt Zoological Society 85
Funnell, Stacey 161

George V, King 2
Gill, Iri 96
Godwin, Mark 95, 112
Golding, Robert (Bob) 58, 61, 62, 106, 139, 157
Golding, Peaches 148, 166
Graves, Barry 46, 104, 105, 111, 137, 140
Greenaway, Ted 65

Hagenbeck, Carl 34
Harris, Rolf 169
Harrison, Stuart 168
Heath, Edward 39
Hervey, William 1, 118
Heythrop Hunt 3
Heyworth, Joanna 57
Heyworth, John *passim.*
Heyworth, Reggie 84, 93, 112, 121, 136
Heyworth, Lt. Colonel Reginald 3
Heyworth, Susan (Sue) 3, 49, 69, 78, 85, 90, 91, 99, 101, 112, 120, 134, 138, 139, 144, 172
Heyworth-Savage, Colonel Cecil Francis 2, 3
Heyworth-Savage, Mrs 3
Hole, Reverend Samuel 120
Holwell 1, 130
Hornsey, Terry 70, 141
Howletts Wild Animal Park 83, 93
Howman, Keith 50
Hughes-Hallet, Michael 13
Hull, Rod 66, 169
Hurley, Ron 70

Injured Jockeys Fund 139
International Herpetological Society 60
ITV 168, 169

James, Norman G 2, 3
'Jinxed' 86
Joiner, Bob 160
Judd, Lesley 146
Junior Friends of Cotswold Wildlife Park 148

Keef, Alan 147
Keep, Sue 130
Kilverstone Hall 72
Knowles, John 6, 28, 46, 48
Knowsley Safari Park 5, 97

Lane, Rachel 137
Lane, Rita 130, 138, 145
Lane, Rod 44, 70, 78, 105, 106, 111, 137, 139, 145
Leeds Castle 108
Lincoln College 84
Lock, Ken 38, 62
London Zoo 38, 45, 93, 121
Longleat Safari Park 4-6, 68, 78, 90
Lord, Colin 31
Lost Gardens of Heligan 121

Mafunyane Game Farm 97
Manley, Eileen 99, 127
Manley, Gerry 37, 101, 102, 129
Manley, Will 37, 44, 101, 102, 107, 109, 129, 136, 139
Manton, Victor 27, 46, 49
Martin, Norma 124, 138, 145

Martin, Richard 38
Martin, Simon 137
Marwell Zoo 4, 6, 7, 28, 46, 48
May, John 32
Mayfield Catering 38
McKenna, Virginia 61
Midwinter, John 51
Miles, Tim 85, 87, 90, 91, 121, 126
Millard, Andy 98
Mitchell, Margaret 119, 120
Molesworth, Michael 51, 151-155, 157, 160
Molesworth, Rosemary 155
Morris, Desmond 56, 146
Morris, Johnny 169

National Trust 131
New Scientist 4
Nine O'Clock News 164
Noakes, John 146

Ogilvie, Major J J 11
Opportunity Knocks 169
Ormond, Marc 87
Oxford Botanic Gardens 33
Oxford Regional Hospital Board 3
Oxfordshire County Council 125, 153, 156

Pace, Richard 2
Packer, John 51
Paignton Zoo 33
Palmer, Mandy 96
Pape, Barry 20
Pauling, Peter 16
Peat, Louise 134
Penscynor Wildlife Park 71
Peper Harow 121
Pertwee, Jon 56
Phipps, George 125
Pickles, Richard 37
Pitelen, George 14, 124
Platt, Nigel 70, 74, 141
Price, Alan 98
Purves, Peter 146

RAF Brize Norton 36
Ravensden Zoological Company 18
Ray, Don 38
Red Poll Cattle Society 43
Reeseheath College 96
Reid, Don 44, 60, 70, 106, 156, 158, 168
Richens, Geoff 126
Rogers, Daphne 76
Royal Agricultural College 11, 64
Royal Engineers, 120
Royal Horticultural Society 32

San Diego Zoo 36
Savile, Jimmy 169
Scarrot, Steve 147
Scotia Investments 4, 28
Scott, Les 13-15, 21, 25, 32, 33, 43, 59, 65, 85, 115, 117, 120, 121, 124-126, 171
Scott, Lillian 116, 142
Scott, Peter 151
Secret World Wildlife Rescue 86
Simmons, John 38, 108
Simpson, Alf 124
Simpson, Sid 14, 124
Sinfield, Ann 12, 21, 34, 131, 136

Sinfield, Brian 12, 15, 16, 19, 20, 23, 30, 31, 35-37, 41, 44, 99, 102, 109, 136, 153, 157, 163, 171
Spicer, Kevin 132
Spooner, Steve 131
Stellingen 34
Stone, John 51, 52, 72, 89, 116, 132, 158, 169
Stourton, Michael 68
Strawberry Hill 1
Sturridge, Piers 131
Styles, Nick 37
Swindon Advertiser 167

Taronga Park 12
Tarrant, Chris 169
Taylor, Bryan 77, 105
Taylor, E, & Son 15
Taylor, John 10, 11, 15, 18, 28, 38, 128
Teer, Isobel 132
Thetford Wildlife Park 12
TISWAS 56, 169
Travers, Bill 61
Twycross Zoo 4, 5, 7, 46, 57, 68

University of Oxford 45

Vickers, John 166
Vincent, Betty 132, 145
Virgin Airlines 141

Walters, Pete 44, 102, 109
Warwick Castle 145
Wax, Ruby 92, 170
Welsh Mountain Zoo 77
West Midlands Zoological Society 56
West Oxfordshire District Council 67
Whipsnade Park Zoo 6, 27, 34, 46, 49
White, Jenny 103
Widdows, Keith 131
Wilks, Dennis 67
Wilks, Doug 67
Williams, Martyn 70, 103, 108
Williams, Philip 66
Windsor Safari Park 13, 36
Witney Gazette 113
Woburn Safari Park 5, 62, 68
Woolham, Mike 70, 109
World Pheasant Association 50, 79
World Wildlife Fund 141, 154, 155

Zoo Check 61, 63
Zoo Licensing Act 63, 157